Regimes of Narcissism,
Regimes of Despair

Regimes of Narcissism,
Regimes of Despair

Ashis Nandy

OXFORD
UNIVERSITY PRESS

OXFORD

UNIVERSITY PRESS

Oxford University Press is a department of the University of Oxford.
It furthers the University's objective of excellence in research, scholarship,
and education by publishing worldwide. Oxford is a registered trademark of
Oxford University Press in the UK and in certain other countries

Published in India by
Oxford University Press
22 Workspace, 2nd Floor, 1/22 Asaf Ali Road, New Delhi 110002, India

First Edition published in 2013
12th impression 2024

ISBN-13: 978-0-19-808965-0
ISBN-10: 0-19-808965-1

Typeset in Arno Pro 12/15.5
by alphæta Solutions, Puducherry, India 605 009
Printed in India by Manipal Technologies Limited, Manipal

Dedicated to the memory of Neelan Thiruchelvam,
Ivan Illich, Michio Araki, and R.L. Kumar—four friends
whose departure has reduced the breadth of my world

Contents

Preface

These essays are about an India that is no longer the country on which I have written for around four decades. Many things have changed drastically in recent years: the mythos on which modern India built its self-definition is under severe stress.

To go by global common sense, the fate of India is being decided by its mainstream politics and dramatic changes in its economic fortunes. But we have seen mighty empires die of unintended implosion, because the mythos on which they leaned had collapsed. The fate of India might be decided not so much by its normal politics or economics but by the large pockets of its political culture that have become the domains of two predominant psychological states: narcissism and despair. To identify their institutionalized forms and inner dynamics, I have begun to call them regimes of narcissism and despair.

Regimes of narcissism are built not only on individual psychopathology, as Christopher Lasch recognized in the late 1970s, but also on political-cultural realities. Regimes of despair, too, may reflect not merely the state of mental health in a society, as some recent psychiatric works on the high incidence of depression in India suggest, but can also be the measure of a cultural crisis from which there is no apparent escape.

The suicides of more than two hundred fifty thousand farmers during the last two decades in India—not in the underdeveloped or backward regions of the country but in places where the success story of Indian agriculture has been written and the Green Revolution was once raucously celebrated—tells a story few Indians want to hear. We feel that we have seen enough poverty and suffering over the years to explore how one of the world's most resilient, autonomous, self-confident peasantries is ceding agency to agronomists, laboratories, market, and the state, and learning to peacefully succumb to despair and self-destruction as its predestined fate. We would rather like to read the story of the billion-dollar house that an Indian, one of the world's richest persons, has built in one of the poorest countries in the world in one of its cruellest cities.

Meanwhile, some psychiatric reports have found fault with the peasants who have killed themselves and, predictably, pleaded for better professional help for those suffering from the sudden epidemic of depression. There are only cursory references in these reports to the desperation of peasants entering a regime of increasingly industrialized and corporatized agriculture, facing the destruction of an entire life-support system and a way of life, and the consequent loss of agency and purpose in life. Strangely, what the knowledge industry in India has often failed to diagnose, some in the much maligned voluntary sector have not failed to notice. They have not gulped the easy explanations floating around in the policy circles; they have sensed that the 4,000-year-old peasant lifestyle in India, which till recently constituted the heart of the Indic civilization, is being pushed into extinction.

A majority of India's roughly 250 tribes, too, now face a new India that wants them to retire into history, vacating space for more spectacular development. They are promised handsome help in their final journey into oblivion from a generation of urban, middle-class India that reads their desperate battle for survival either as an ideological battle waged by a group of hare-brained radicals or as atavistic resistance to a progress that now comes in the guise of mega-technology and the global market. The role these communities have played in defining India's cultural identity, creativity, and dignity has been rewritten as only a history of underdevelopment, poverty, and exploitation.

The tribal communities of the whole of South Asia since the Mahabharata times—I stand by this anti-historical chronology—have collectively served as a counter-player or nec-essary double of the 'eternal India' that we have known and cel-ebrated. Pushed into destitution, marginalized, and denied even a vestige of dignity by modern India, many tribes have now become targets of a new form of double displacement.

First, there is the territorial displacement of communities from their traditional habitat. Turning overnight into floating populations of the disinherited and the disposable, they become a part of the country's new proletariat and survive as tribes only on official papers. Second, the tribes have become victims of the psychological defence of displacement built into the political cul-ture of modern India. Once the target of the civilizing mission of colonialism, large sections of India's policy elite have internalized their former rulers and have displaced the distaste for their own non-modern self towards those who have lost or opted out of the rat race to beat the West at its own game. It is the new brown man's burden and it includes a new psychological equation: tribal India today is what we were yesterday and their tomorrow is nothing other than what we are today. The culture of India's urban middle-class is being re-engineered to accommodate the mission.

Even some of the more ardent, self-proclaimed well-wishers of the tribes can think of no better deal for them than 'proletarian-ization'. Only in scattered literary and artistic works—infrequently in cinema—one finds their sorrows, suffering, happiness, and hopes reflected as fragments of a slightly premature epitaph. Not surprisingly, it has taken an art historian, Harsha Dehejia, to announce the entry of despair as a rasa into our contemporary arts. It was never one of the nine rasas mentioned in classical aesthetic theory.

☙

Regimes of narcissism at some points have to meet regimes of despair. Anyone who has followed the career of the concept of narcissism in psychoanalysis and psychiatry knows that narcissism has never been a matter of plain self-centredness or eroticized egotism. It usually has as its underside incapacitating self-doubts and feelings of inferiority. The overt certitudes and the overdone investment in self cover up for these doubts and the gnawing absence of self-esteem. Ideological closures and narrowing of emotional range are often easy ways out of this inner tension. A billion-dollar house at a metropolis is never an adequate compensation for the memories of early years of struggle of one's family, the social insecurities and private anxieties, and the ethical compromises one had to make in a system demanding such compromises at every step, in the name of hard-eyed realism or tough-minded competition. A billion-dollar house is a desperate affirmation that one has survived. It is a denial of mortality, not through the gambit of great creativity or heroic interventions in society and politics, but by playing chess with the demons of obscure, dreary ordinariness and lonely death.

A few years before Lasch, the now-forgotten political activist and writer Philip Spratt drew upon psychoanalysis to propose that the culture of Hinduism sanctioned a form of narcissism that gave a distinctive tone to Indian public life. At that time

Spratt's diagnosis seemed an easy Freudian fling to many but, in retrospect, one is tempted to read it as an early response to the same double-edged nature of social change that binds the two regimes in a passionate embrace.

The regimes of narcissism and despair also meet when the expanding global middle-class culture tries to normalize the narcissism and medicalize the despair. When the effort succeeds, it looks like a perfect fit between the two and a manageable part of a global project, in which one regime becomes the certified caretaker of the other. A formidable set of psychological defences protect the regimes of narcissism and begin to impute the nastiest motives to those who see narcissism as a sickness, not as part of normality. The desperate and others perturbed by their desperation are given a different set of defences. They begin to look at their desperation as a contagious disease, resulting from the vulnerability to the normal stress of living in a globalized political economy, not as a heightened sensitivity to a core crisis of politics.

A special case of the normalization of narcissism is the pedagogic role assumed by the regimes of narcissism. For, they have declared themselves the future of the rest of us. If they can do what they have done, everyone else can do so too, unless they are lazy, non-enterprising, and dismissive towards their betters. Every theory of progress, social-evolutionary design for development, or chronology of historical stages, whatever its ideological roots, can be read as a desperate bid to bolster the defences of narcissism and to reconfirm its status as the new opiate of the privileged.

This book does not tell the story that this preface seemingly promises. But it might not have been written without an awareness of the issues raised here. I do touch upon in this book on the way the inner world of a civilization is being engineered to match the expectations of the dominant global climate of opinion. This has been a theme in many of my earlier writings on mass violence and macro-political interventions in our times— interventions based on secular master narratives offering what many believe are hard, inescapable, fool-proof, quasi-scientific laws of political economy and history. Just because the language of positive sciences has given way to the language of herme-neutics, the need to have certitudes has not weakened. At one time, the forerunners of these narratives offered revealed laws of nature and human nature. They have been discarded in recent centuries as forms of primitivism. In their place have come a new set of public myths, in the guise of immutable laws of per-petual progress.

The fate of superseded theories is well-known in the natu-ral sciences. They are treated as lovable foibles of a more inno-cent age or as milestones on a road no longer used except by the historians of science. These dead theories are almost fully dead. In social knowledge, theories have a longer life. Many of them survive for a century or two; others live longer. Also, they often wait patiently for decades for new fans and new preys like hungry carnivores. New generations with short memories and blunted scepticism are their easy victims. These theories do ultimately die but, in the meanwhile, the collateral damages they inflict are fearsome.

Social theories live longer when they are used as ideologies. But the high priests of ideologies also suspect that the theories framing their ideologies may not be, after all, immortal. They have to be kept alive or resurrected for the new generations. That does not make the ideologues more tentative, but less. Their own fantasies of immortality are predicated on the immor-tality of their theories. The suspicion of their mortality makes them doubly insecure and more insistent on conformity and more ruthless with dissent. Ideologies and ideologues tend to become genocidal in our times. Often the change comes slowly and with small initiatives in obscure places that produce, almost by default, a polarization of positions. Environmentalist Aseem Srivastava tells me that in the small town called Kudankulam in Tamil Nadu, which most Indians did not know existed before an anti-nuclear movement broke out there a few months ago, cases of sedition have been filed against roughly 3,000 men and women, most of them living below the poverty line.

In my earlier writings there were criticisms of specific ideologies, not of ideologies as such. I now sense within me a growing discomfort with ideologies themselves as a class of belief systems. (I am not speaking of ideologies the way Karl Marx and Karl Mannheim spoke of them, but the way psychoanalysts and political psychologists study them, as vectors in the inner life of a person.) The source of my discomfort lies in the accumulating empirical data, which show that in the last hundred years the secular political ideologies have taken a much higher toll of human lives than religious fanaticism, though the situation in earlier centuries might have been very different. I also notice that the resistance to the pathologies of ideology tend to be more robust at the ground level, especially in community-based societies of the South. For, the commitment to ideologies is mostly skin-deep in such societies, and social relations and basic human values are seen as more important.

As in most of my recent works, this collection of essays, too, seeks to open up the future for the next generation of intellectuals and political activists in India and in other societies facing similar choices. It is my hope that they will feel less constrained by the certitudes of my generation and make writings likes these redundant.

ॐ

Most essays in this book began as formal lectures. 'Nationalism, Genuine and Spurious' is a much revised version of the 3rd Usha Mehta Memorial Lecture at the Nehru Centre, Mumbai, in 2005 which was published in the *Economic and Political Weekly*, 12 August 2006, and, then, with further revisions, in the *Ashis Nandy Reader* (Shanghai: West Heavens Project and Nanfang Daily Press, 2010). I am grateful to Bhikhu Parekh, chairing the lecture, for his detailed, extremely useful comments. The present version also owes much to Sandip Bandopadhyay who, while translating it into Bengali, pointed out a number of errors in the earlier text.

'The Demonic and the Seductive in Religious Nationalism' began as a brief paper written for Michio Araki at the 19th World Congress of the International Association for the History of Religions, Tokyo, in 2005. An expanded version became the Sankari Prasad Bannerjee Memorial Lecture at the Department of Philosophy, Calcutta University, in 2006 and a lecture at the Ruprecht-Karls-Universität, Heidelberg, in 2008. A part of the latter version was published on the website of the Karl Jaspers Centre of the University. The version in this book was written for Asian Circle of Thought at the Inter-Asia School at Shanghai. I am grateful to Suresh Sharma and Subrata Mitra for facilitating the writing of this essay and to Siegfried O. Wolf, who introduced me to little-known materials on Savarkar's sojourn at London.

'Coming Home' began as a lecture at the 25th Anniversary of International Centre for Ethnic Studies in 2008 and was later presented in a conference on Gandhi in a Globalized World, at the Central European University the same year. An Open Society Fellowship at Budapest facilitated the work. The paper uses data from a larger study of the mass violence that accompanied the birth of India and Pakistan as independent states. This work could not have been done without the help and collaboration of Rajni Bakshi, journalist and activist-scholar. Also, Dilip Gaonkar supplied some excellent critical comments when a version of the paper was published in *Public Culture* in Spring 2011.

The origins of 'Return of the Sacred' lie in a serial trialogue that took place among Michio Araki, Charles Long, and me at a number of Japanese universities during 2005–6. That intellectual exchange has remained a memorable and formative influence in me. The present version specifically draws upon the Mahesh Chandra Regmi Lecture at Kathmandu in 2007 and the C.R. Parekh Lecture at the University of Westminster, London, in 2008.

'Terror, Counter-terror, and Self-destruction' began as a keynote address at the International Symposium on Cultural Diversity and Information Network at Tokyo, organized by Tamotsu Aoki and Masako Okamoto for the National Graduate Institute for Policy Studies in 2001. It was also presented at a symposium 'Edward Said: Speaking Truth to Power', organized by the Institute for Research and Development in Humanities, Tarbiyat Modaress University, Tehran University, and the Center for Dialogue of Civilizations in Tehran in 2004. The symposium was the initiative of Ramin Jahanbegloo. The present version was written for Michalis S. Michael and Fabio Petito (eds), *Civilizational Dialogue and World Order: The Other Politics of Cultures, Religions, and Civilizations in International Relations* (New York: Palgrave Macmillan, 2009, pp. 167–80).

'Humiliation' was presented at a conference organized by the Centre for the Study of Developing Societies and the Nirman Foundation. The conference proceedings were published as Gopal Guru (ed.), *Humiliation, Claims and Context* (New Delhi: Oxford University Press, 2009).

'Modernity and the Sense of Loss' grew out of public lectures at Jamia Millia Islamia, New Delhi, and GTZ, Berlin in 2004. The present version was written for the West Heavens Project: India–China Summit on Social Thought and the 8th Shanghai Biennale in 2010 and was published in *Inter-Asia Cultural Studies*, 12(3), 2011.

'Happiness' was delivered as the 13th Kappen Memorial Lecture at Bangalore on 22 September 2011. It has grown out of a brief trialogue among Tamotsu Aoki, Nur Yalman, and me, organized some years ago by Iwanami Shoten in Tokyo. The discussion spilt into a conference on Culture and Hegemony: Politics of Culture in the Age of Globalization, organized by GRIPS project of the University of Tokyo and by the Institut fur Ethnologie, Ruprecht-Karls-Universität, Heidelberg, and into a short article published in Spanish in a yearbook. The present version was first published in *Economic and Political Weekly*, 47(2), 14 January 2012.

ASHIS NANDY
January 2013

N ationalism, Genuine and Spurious

A Very Late Obituary of Two Early Post–nationalist Strains in India

Indians, Vinay Lal tells us, are inveterate record seekers.[1] From no other country does the *Guinness World Records* receive so many applications for recognition. At least one-tenth of all applications that it receives emanate from India—and some of them do get into the book—from the silent holy man who stayed on the same spot on a roadside in a village for twenty-two years to someone who wrote 1,314 characters on a single grain of rice to set a record in microwriting.[2] Strangely, the record that the Indians have *not* claimed is a unique one; it involves an achievement that has not been equalled in the 350-year-long history of nation-states and is unlikely to be

---

[1] Vinay Lal, *Of Cricket, Guinness and Gandhi: Essays on Indian History and Culture* (Calcutta: Seagull, 2003), pp. 1–22; see pp. 2, 4–5.
[2] Ibid.

broken till the nation-state system survives. Rabindranath Tagore (1861–1941), by common consent India's national poet, who has written and scored India's national anthem, *Jana Gana Mana*, is also the composer of India's national song, *Vande Mataram*, written by Bankimchandra Chattopadhyay (1838–1894). Tagore also happens to be the writer and composer of the national anthem of Bangladesh. In recent years, anti-India sentiments have grown in Bangladesh and there is also a budding fundamentalist movement in the country, hostile to everything Indian or Hindu. Yet, not one voice has been raised, to the best of my knowledge, against the national anthem written by Tagore. That is not all. Tagore has also scored Sri Lanka's national anthem, though he has not written the lyric. Sri Lankans, too, may not always live happily with the Indian state, but they seem to live happily with India's national poet.

Tagore is not alone; there are other less dramatic instances of the same kind. I could mention here the song *Sare Jahan se Accha* of Mohammad Iqbal (1877–1938), the national poet and one of the founding fathers of Pakistan, which constitutes the main marching song of the Indian army, even when it marches to fight the Pakistan army. Pakistan's first national anthem, too, was written by a Hindu, Jagan Nath Azad (1918–2004), at the invitation of Mohammad Ali Jinnah (1876–1948), Pakistan's father of nation. Obviously, the concepts of territoriality and 'national culture' work trifle differently in South Asia.

After he won the Nobel Prize in 1913, Tagore became a pan-Asian hero. He was the first Asian to win a Nobel Prize in any subject and he did so in the high noon of colonialism. That mattered. In 1916, when World War I was raging in Europe, Tagore went to Japan for the first time on a lecture tour. When he arrived at Kobe, the Japanese welcomed him warmly. At some places, he was treated like a monarch on a state visit and his movements were reported on front pages of some Japanese newspapers.

Unfortunately, some of the lectures Tagore delivered were on nationalism. Today, they may not seem disturbingly radical; while some of the arguments are now familiar, others seem remarkably fresh and provocative.[3] But none of them is likely to set the Bay of Tokyo on fire. However, at the time most Japanese were in the throes of a rather delirious version of nationalism; they found Tagore's critique of nationalism terribly disconcerting. Not only were there in the lectures a severe indictment of militarism and imperialism inspired by nationalism, there were in them snide comments on Japan's newly forged political self centring on the idea of European-style nationalism. What was dangerous for Japan, Tagore insisted, was 'not the imitation of the outer features of the West, but acceptance of the motive force of the Western nationalism as her own.'[4] Embarrassed and angry, most Japanese newspapers and intellectuals wrote-off the lectures as the ramblings of a poet from a defeated civilization (as some Chinese were to do for a different set of reasons, when Tagore visited China in 1924). Basking in Japan's newfound imperial glory and its success as a new global power, they found Tagore to be a pain in the neck. When Tagore had arrived at Tokyo railway station, thousands came to welcome him. When he was leaving Japan, it is said, only one person came to see him off—his host.[5]

Nationalism was not in short supply in colonial India either. Many Indians also found Tagore's behaviour strange, though

[3] Rabindranath Tagore, *On Nationalism* (1917) (Madras: Macmillan, 1930).
[4] Ibid., pp. 77–8.
[5] For a detailed, useful introduction to criticisms of Tagore in Japan, China, and India, see Stephen Hay, *Asian Ideas of East and West: Tagore and His Critics in Japan, China and India* (Cambridge, Mass.: Harvard University Press, 1970); also, Sisir Kumar Das, 'The Controversial Guest: Tagore in China', in Tan Chung (ed.), *Across the Himalayan Gap: An Indian Quest for Understanding China* (New Delhi: Indira Gandhi National Centre for the Arts, 1998), http://ignca.nic.in/ks_41037.htm.

not inexplicable or unexpected. Their response to the poet was in many ways compatible with the response to him in Japan and China.[6] He had already antagonized hard-boiled Indian nationalists by rejecting the idea of nationalist violence; they were prepared to expect the worst from him. Three of his novels—*Gora* (1909), *Ghare Baire* (1916), and *Char Adhyay* (1934)—were seen as direct attacks on hard-edged, masculine nationalism. They hurt the sentiments of many who had to gulp them for reasons of political correctness. For, paradoxically, Tagore was already India's unofficial national poet. He had written hundreds of patriotic songs that were an inspiration to many participants in India's freedom struggle—from Mohandas Karamchand Gandhi (1869–1948) to humble volunteers and protesters facing police batons and bullets. Even in jail, many freedom fighters kept up their spirits by singing Tagore's songs.

ço

This is not as inconsistent as it seems. There are two clues to how Tagore reconciled his two selves in his works. First, in his Bengali writings, Tagore used something like twelve to fifteen expressions to denote one's love for one's country—ranging from *deshabhiman* and *swadeshprem* to *deshbhakti* and *swadesh-chetana*. But he used none of them as a synonym or translation of the word 'nationalism'. When he meant nationalism he used the English words 'nation' and 'nationalism' in Bengali script to

[6] Private correspondence between the novelist Saratchandra Chattopadhyay and writer-musician Dilip Kumar Roy reveals that many of the young revolutionaries of Bengal, serving long jail sentences for their participation in the freedom struggle, eagerly awaited the publication of the national poet's *Char Adhyay* and were deeply hurt and felt betrayed by Tagore's stance on nationalism, particularly its violent version.

distinguish it from the first set of words. Tagore was a patriot but not a nationalist. He thought there was nothing in common between the territoriality associated with the various vernacular concepts of patriotism and the new idea of territoriality grounded in the idea of nation-state and ideology of nationalism. I suspect that he thought the former to be tied to the idea of home and the latter to be an artificial concoction that looked instrumentally at the former and, indeed, was often built on the ruins of the former. Indeed, nationalism was partly a reaction to a sense of being uprooted or rendered homeless.

Tagore's understanding of nationalism—that is, its genuine European version that took its final shape in the nineteenth century as an inseparable adjunct of the modern nation-state and the idea of nationality—is explicit in a number of essays and letters, but the most moving and disturbing exploration of the social and ethical ramifications of the idea is in his three political novels: *Gora, Ghare Baire*, and *Char Adhyay*. Each of the novels is built around a significant political formulation, though it is doubtful if the poet did so deliberately. In *Gora*, Tagore gives a powerful psychological definition of nationalism where nationalism becomes a defence against recognizing the permeable or porous boundaries of one's self that the cultures in his part of the world sanction. He, in effect, argues that the idea of nationalism is intrinsically non-Indian or anti-Indian, an offence against Indian civilization and its principles of religious and cultural plurality. *Ghare Baire* is a story of how nationalism dismantles community life and releases the demon of ethnoreligious violence. It destroys the 'home' by tinkering with the moral basis of social and cultural reciprocity and hospitality in the Indic civilization. *Char Adhyay* is an early, perhaps the first, exploration of the roots of industrialized, assembly-line violence as a specialization of the modern times. It anticipates the works of Hannah Arendt, Robert J. Lifton, and

Zygmunt Bauman on the changing nature of organized mass violence and its links with nationalism.[7]

Each of the three novels can also be read as a charged, almost obsessive, conversation with his close friend Brahmabandhav Upadhyay (1861–1907), the Catholic theologian and Vedantist who, arguably and paradoxically, was India's first modern, Hindu-nationalist activist-scholar and the first to articulate a theory of aggressive Hindu nationalism, though there are also in the novels arguments with Vivekananda, Nivedita, and perhaps even Rudyard Kipling. Tagore scatters in the personalities of the heroes and the anti-heroes of the novels Upadhyay's and his own fears, anxieties, hopes, and visions as well as aspects of their selves and anti-selves.[8]

The second clue comes from Tagore's understanding of the cultural unity of India. Unlike many others in his and ours times, Tagore believed that the canonical texts of India—the Vedas, the Upanishads, and the Gita—might be at the centre of India's classical culture but they do not constitute the heart of Indian unity or provide the basis of it. Here he differs radically from the likes of Rammohun Roy, Swami Vivekananda, Sri Aurobindo, and an array of eminent nineteenth-century thinkers who believed that the canonical texts of Hinduism defined the basis of Indianness. Indian unity, Tagore insists, is built on the thoughts and practices of the medieval mystics, poets, and religious and

---

[7] Hannah Arendt, *Eichmann in Jerusalem* (New York: Viking, 1963); Robert J. Lifton, *Nazi Doctors: Medical Killings and the Psychology of Genocide* (New York: Basic Books, 1986); Zygmunt Bauman, *Modernity and the Holocaust* (Ithaca, New York: Cornell University, 1989).

[8] On the complex relationship between Tagore and Upadhyay, both as persons and as theorists of nationalism, see Ashis Nandy, *The Illegitimacy of Nationalism: Rabindranath Tagore and the Politics of Self* (New Delhi: Oxford University Press, 1994).

spiritual figures.[9] In such a country, importing the Western concept of nationalism was like Switzerland trying to build a navy.[10]

This must have been a terribly painful position for Tagore to take. He was a Brahmo and belonged to a family that had been at the forefront of the nineteenth-century reform movements within Hinduism. The Brahmos made it a point to deploy the so-called uncontaminated, canonical, sacred texts of India like the Vedas and the Upanishads to fight for social reform among the Hindus—to oppose sati, fight untouchability, promote widow remarriage, and battle child marriage. Tagore's stance negated a part of his own inheritance and self. It also militated against the entrenched belief of a large proportion of India's modern elite, influenced by the three major nineteenth-century reform movements in Hinduism—Brahmo Samaj, Arya Samaj, and Ramakrishna Mission—that the Vedas, the Upanishads, and the Gita enshrined a more rational strand in Indian traditions and could be the main means of fighting the deformities of Hinduism that seemingly derived sanction from the less canonical strands of traditions.

On the other hand, Tagore's position opened up the possibility of viewing India as a relatively more fluid, less rigidly bordered cultural entity defined by a number of mystics and saints, the boundaries of whose religious identities were never exactly clear. Like Kabir, Nanak, Bulleh Shah, and Lalan, they could simultaneously belong to more than one religious tradition. Also, this way of defining India's oneness partly dissociated Indianness from the state and allowed some degree of scepticism towards the ideology of a national state, an ideology towards which modern India was already showing a certain fondness.[11] Tagore was

[9] Tagore, On Nationalism, p. 64.
[10] Ibid., p. 65.
[11] Partha Chatterjee is uncomfortable with this formulation. Tagore was not against the idea of the state, he suggests. 'Ravindrik Nation Ki', Sunil Kumar

seeking to clearly separate patriotism from nationalism so as to create an intellectual and psychological base that would allow the 'natural' territoriality of a political community to avoid getting metastasized into European-style nationalism. He knew the record of European nationalism within Europe and in the southern hemisphere and he foresaw the devastation towards which European nationalism was pushing Europe and the world.

Even though they sometimes differed radically on public issues, Tagore was a friend and admirer of Gandhi. He was the first person to call Gandhi a Mahatma and invited Gandhi to take care of his alternative university at Shantiniketan after his death. He made Gandhi a trustee of Shantiniketan. Gandhi reciprocated these sentiments and was the first person to call Tagore Gurudev, a teacher-god. He also shared Tagore's belief that Indian unity was primarily a product of medieval, not classical, India. His dismissive comments on iconic nineteenth-century religious reformers like Rammohun Roy and their religious reform movements, all of which tried to return to the canonical texts, reflect that agreement. It is not surprising that though he started from an entirely different intellectual vantage ground, Gandhi's concept of nationalism at one point converged with that of Tagore. Those who have read or even glimpsed at the hundred-volume *The Collected Works of Mahatma Gandhi* know that the references to nationalism in them are sparse.[12] Most of these mentions are critical and seek to differentiate it from its European namesake. Gandhi was always

---

Sen Memorial Lecture, *Baromas*, Annual Puja No., 2003, pp. 7–25. May be Tagore was not, but if we do not conflate the idea of the state with that of the nation-state, Tagore obviously could not be particularly fond of the idea of the nation-state, given that such a state cannot be dissociated from nation and nationalism, which are expected to act as its binding cement.

[12] M.K. Gandhi, *The Collected Works of Mahatma Gandhi* (New Delhi: Publications Division, Government of India).

keen to define his nationalism as part of a universal struggle for justice and equality and he made it clear, in so many words, that the other name for armed nationalism was imperialism and he considered it a curse.[13] Gandhi may be the official father of the Indian nation, but he was hardly a genuine nationalist. He was mainly an uncompromising anti-imperialist. His much-maligned ultra-nationalist assassin, Nathuram Godse, understood this part of the story much better than many Gandhians did and acted upon it.

ᴄᴏ

I am walking dangerous grounds. Not only have I drawn attention to the eccentric hostility of our national poet to the idea of nationalism, I have diagnosed the nationalism of the father of the nation as fraudulent. Worse, I have read his assassin's nationalism as the genuine stuff, grounded in dominant contemporary ideas of sanity and rationality. Please note, however, that I have not accused these two tallest figures of contemporary India of being unpatriotic. For those who think that nationalism and patriotism are the same, I consider it my responsibility to spell out here, even if at the cost of simplification, the differences between nationalism and what, in the absence of a better term, I have called patriotism.[14]

---

[13] Ibid., Vol. 25, p. 369.

[14] I am aware that in countries like the United States and France the borderline between nationalism and patriotism has been traditionally blurry, so that the terms are often used interchangeably. To some extent, this is true of much of South Asia too. At one time this did not matter. I am here trying to draw a clear line between the two because, with the quickening pace of modernization and integration into a global system, we are getting the purer, copy-book instance of nationalism and have begun to pay for the consequences. Political theory demands that we make this analytic distinction at this point of time.

To talk of the obvious first, patriotism is an emotional state, bonding, or investment; it is a sentiment. Non-specific, non-ideological territoriality—of the kind seen even in many species of non-human mammals and in some species of birds and insects—is the basis of patriotism. Such feelings of territoriality are seen as natural to human beings, both by those who share the feelings and those who claim that they do not.

Nationalism is an ideology. Not in the sense in which Karl Marx and Karl Mannheim defined the term ideology but in the sense in which social and political psychologists use the term—as an identifiable pattern of attitudes, beliefs, values, and needs in human personality. Even those who use the term 'nationalism' without caring about its ideological contents, end up imbibing some of the contents. This is because they have to constantly interact with those who carry the ideological baggage of nationalism and are affected by such consensual validation. Nationalism, thus, is more specific, ideologically tinged, ardent form of 'love of one's own kind' that is essentially ego-defensive and overlies some degree of fearful dislike or positive hostility to 'outsiders'. It is ego-defensive because it is often a reaction to the inner, unacknowledged fears of atomization or psychological homelessness induced by the weakening or dissolution of primordial ties and growing individuation, alienating work, and the death of vocations, in turn brought about by technocratic capitalism, urbanization, and industrialization. Often such nationalism is honed by the uprooting—and the consequent sense of loss—that urbanization and development bring about.

On this plane, nationalism is a compensatory mechanism. It supplies in the form of a nation a pseudo-community, as Hannah Arendt once named it, or an imaginary community, as Benedict Anderson has described it at greater length. Patriotism, on the other hand, presumes the existence of communities other than the country and gives them due recognition, sometimes even priority. It is at least vaguely aware that there can be contradictions between the demands of the nation and of these communities. Unlike nationalism, patriotism makes no claim that the ideal relationship between the individual and the state is an unmediated one.

Second, nationalism is also partly a response to the awareness that the world is dominated by and organized around nation-states and the rules of international diplomacy and power play have been framed keeping nation-states in mind. Survival in such a world demands knowledge of these rules, skills in handling them, and some ease with the culture of nation-states. A degree of statism is, thus, an unavoidable adjunct of nationalism.[15]

Patriotism makes no such presumption or demand. Being a sentiment, it does not have to be organized around the concept of a national state. Even when the state becomes central in some situations, as for instance when a country faces attack and patriotic feelings are roused, that centrality is transient and has a clear instrumental touch.

Also, unlike nationalism, which demands a uniform allegiance or loyalty to the state, patriotism can live with different levels of

---

[15] When contemporary India's best-known theorist of Hindu nationalism, Vinayak Damodar Savarkar (1883–1966)—scholar, poet, revolutionary, and the real inspirer of Gandhi's assassination—accused Gandhi of being 'unscientific' and 'unscholarly', it was not merely because of Brahminic contempt for what to Savarkar looked like amateurish political thought, it was also because of the widely shared fear in India's modernizing elite that Gandhi was flouting the canons of modern political theory and statecraft. See Ashis Nandy, 'The Demonic and the Seductive in Religious Nationalism: Vinayak Damodar Savarkar and the Rites of Exorcism in Secularizing South Asia', in this book and 'The Lure of "Normal" Politics: Gandhi and the Battle for Popular Culture of Politics in India', *South Asian Popular Culture*, October 2007, 5(2), pp. 167–78.

loyalty, affiliation, and allegiance to the state. The relationship between the state and patriotism is open to bargaining. Some may show allegiance by paying a substantive or nominal tribute, others by contributing to the state's army, still others by granting certain one-sided privileges to those controlling the state.[16] This also means that patriotism can probably bring together people for a particular cause only by creating something close to a consensus in the society. And that consensus is usually issue-specific. For instance, the anti-imperial sentiment that patriotism breeds is not automatically driven by dreams of homogenized nation-states that would mimic the imperial states in all respects, except that the rulers of these future states would come from among the former colonial subjects.

In sum, the crucial premise of nationalism is that the state is central to public life, if not to life itself. In postcolonial societies, nationalism usually works with a popular, lowbrow version of the Hegelian idea of the state, picked up from the global culture of common sense. Patriotism may or may not be statist, but it is usually less uncomfortable with civil society. The state enters the picture as a distant player in day-to-day life.

[16] The Mughal and Ottoman empires were reasonably good examples of what I have in mind. It is by following the conventions of the Mughal Empire that the British-Indian Empire, too, allowed some degree of differentiation in alliance to the Empire. It can be argued that the Cabinet Mission plan envisaged a similar arrangement for independent India. So did, many have now begun to suspect, Mohammed Ali Jinnah, as opposed to the more 'progressive' statists in the Indian National Congress, seeking a powerful, highly centralized, unitary state in tune with then-fashionable socialist dogmas. That the Indian state gradually came to resemble what Arend Lijphart was to later call a 'consociational state' is a different story. See, for example, Arend Lijphart, *Democracies: Patterns of Majoritarian and Consensus Government in Twenty-One Countries* (New Haven: Yale University Press, 1984); and *Patterns of Democracy: Government Forms and Performance in Thirty Six Countries* (New Haven: Yale University Press, 1999).

Third, nationalism insists on the primacy of national identity over identities built on subnational allegiances—religions, castes, sects, linguistic affiliations, and ethnicities. It promotes decontextualized formulae or slogans like 'we are Indians first, then Hindus, Tamils or Dalits'. For nationalism expects all identities to be subservient to the interests of the national state. As a general rule, nationalism fears other identities as potential rivals and subversive presences. Patriotism does not automatically demand such primacy; on the whole, the state is expected to serve the needs of society and culture, not the other way round.

Fourth, it follows from the earlier three propositions that nationalism presumes some degree of modernity. Patriotism does not make this presumption and, as we all know, it has flourished in premodern times and in non-modern societies. To that extent, it is more open to a post-nationalist, postmodern world. One suspects that the survival of communities and a modicum of popular suspicion towards unbridled individualism are essential for non-nationalist forms of patriotism to prosper. As a form of territoriality, patriotism works with a concept of 'home' that could be a country but could also be a region, city, or a village.

However, to complete the picture, one must add that, beyond a point, modernity and individuation begin to blunt the edge of nationalism, when the middle classes continue to theoretically love nationalism but also begin to see it as a needless constraint on the pursuit of individual self-interest and—what is probably a relatively new development—on socially sanctioned hedonism. It is not surprising that China and India are today two of the most fiercely nationalistic countries in the world despite the frequent laments of their rulers that their citizens are not nationalistic enough. Neither modernization nor individuation is 'complete' in these societies.

Fifth, nationalism, being an ideology, has a positive content, to which the nationalist must conform. That content may sometimes be loosely defined and also may allow some leeway but it is always there. Hence, there is ample scope in nationalism for identifying deviants and traitors and for witch hunts. Patriotism is relatively content-free; it does not clearly benchmark the features of a patriot. It is a fluid form of territoriality, which probably is more open to the idea that it could be the last resort of a scoundrel.[17]

This also means that in South Asia, nationalism as an ideology has a thin presence in most citizens. Not only are the religions alive and kicking in this part of the world, so are many aspects of the traditional cosmologies aligned or associated with religions. You can draw your gods and saints, demons and witches from these cosmologies and do not have to adore or hunt them according to the fiats of nationalism or, for that matter, any ideology. Nationalism at this level is a viable ideological entity mainly in the small minority of urban, educated, modern citizen in whom the principles of the older ways of life have become shaky. This probably explains the spectacular oscillations in South Asian public life between short periods of ardent, maniacal nationalism and equally ardent defiance or neglect of the core tenets of nationalism.

Sixth, nationalism, being an ideology, has to have not merely an identifiable content but also a theoretical frame, however

[17] This is not an attempt to give to patriotic sentiments. I am trying to spell out the distinct organizational principles of a state of mind called nationalism. To do so, one must disentangle the two concepts and be aware that many when they talk of patriotism have in mind nationalism and vice versa. Everyone knows the bloody record of patriotism in premodern times and non-modern societies. Few seem alert to the way anxieties and fears associated with territoriality have been given a particular slant in contemporary times under the global nation-state system, the way a natural human instinct like aggression is given an unnatural form in wars and genocide.

coarse and repetitious. That frame includes a set of ends and means; a series of propositions on national culture and national community, their origins and differentia, and an idea of national interest that supersedes the interests of aggregates larger and smaller than the nation. These are seen as the building blocks of an existing or potential nation-state. In the southern hemisphere, particularly among its modern elite, certain magical qualities are imputed to this frame, which is seen as crucial clues to the West's power and success. The culture of common sense in the global middle class does not go that far but it does see nationalism as an inescapable part of a modern nation-state. Even the critics of nationalism, including many who see it as an unmitigated evil, usually believe it to be an unavoidable stage in a country's political life.

This theoretical frame of nationalism turns nationalism into a homogenizing force and into a house-broken version of patriotism in a modern state. In this respect the career of nationalism in our times runs parallel to that of the ideology of secularism. The role of the ideology of secularism, too, is to produce docile, manageable versions of religions with which the modern state can easily establish a quid pro quo.

Finally and most importantly, nationalism follows the iron law associated with all ideologies, Marxism to developmentalism and feminism to Hindutva: nationalism has at its core, at best discomfort or ambivalence, at worst contempt for its targeted beneficiaries. From the left Hegelian discomfort with the masses that seem insufficiently revolutionary to Hindutva's contempt for the Hindus who seem inadequately masculine, martial, and organized, it is the same story. Nationalists are always nervous that the nation is not nationalistic enough, that it is gullible about its own interests and security needs, insensitive to humiliation, and ever unwilling to actualize its full potentialities. Hence, the more the nationalists come to love the abstract entity called the nation, the more they dislike the real-life persons and communities that constitute the nation.[18] The frequent witch hunts that the ultra-nationalists mount are a direct outcome of this ambivalence.

જી

Let me end the story by reaffirming that two of the tallest figures in twentieth-century India looked forward to a postcolonial India that would also simultaneously be post-nationalist. They might not have worded their critiques this way but that is because the political vocabulary available to them was narrower. It is true that some of their writings allow a casual reader to classify them as nationalists—official India has already done so and got away with it—they both were at best imperfect or bad nationalists. To call them nationalists is to vend a local, vernacular version of territoriality, a patently ersatz nationalism.

One issue has remained unresolved. If patriotism is a pre-ideological state of mind, closer to our biological self, and nationalism is an ideology, nationalism should be more space-bound and time-bound. Yet, the content of nationalism has shown very little variation over cultural and geographical borders. Probably this has something to do with Europe's triumphant presence in the southern hemisphere during the high noon of nationalism in the second half of the nineteenth century and the first half of the twentieth. For all we know, nationalism outside Europe might

---

[18] Perhaps the most extreme example of this split is Adolf Hitler's last testament where he insisted that the German people did not deserve to survive because they had proven themselves weaker than the people of the East. One finds shades of such attitudes in a number of Hindu nationalist texts, notably in V.D. Savarkar's works, who believed that only Europeanized Hindus operating as a proper textbook instance of a nationality could fulfil their destiny.

have taken a different shape if it was not seen in the South as a universal, modern technology—by many as a European magic— that had to be mastered to beat Europe at its own game. Early in its life, nationalism became part of the social-evolutionist baggage exported to and internalized by the defeated civilizations.

Fortunately for the Indian nationalists, secular or otherwise, the evil influence of the two maverick thinkers I have discussed is now waning. We are now proudly moving towards the genuine stuff—the real, textbook version of nationalism about which Ernest Gellner once said that you do not have to examine its contents in different parts of the world, for they are always the same.[19] That implies, paradoxically, nationalist thought is never nationally distinctive; it is globalized by definition. And it was so decades before globalization became a buzz word. A recent survey in forty-four countries shows the Indians to be the most nationalistic in the world. To please Indian nationalists, it is now more nationalistic than Pakistan, the United States, and the United Kingdom.[20] Both Tagore and Gandhi, if they were living, might have felt this to be a prescription for disaster but, fortunately, they are dead. Indeed, to spite them, the clones of proudly nationalist nuclear scientists A.Q. Khan and Raja Ramanna are swarming all over South Asia. Who cares about two effete, wishy-washy, woolly-headed dreamers driven by cultural nostalgia and a foolishly uncritical, romanticized view of India's past as a resource for its future?

[19] Ernest Gellner, *Nations and Nationalism* (Ithaca, New York: Cornell University Press, 1983).
[20] Pramit Pal Chaudhuri, 'Poll Shows Indians are Most Nationalistic', *Hindustan Times*, 8 June 2003. The column is based on the results of the Pew Global Attitudes Project, which collected data from forty-four countries, including Pakistan, the United States, Bangladesh, and the United Kingdom. For more details, see Pew Global Attitudes Project, *Views of a Changing World*, Chapter 5, 'Nationalism, Sovereignty and Views of Global Institutions', http:// pewrsr.ch/VrML9v.

The Demonic and the Seductive in Religious Nationalism

Vinayak Damodar Savarkar and the Rites of Exorcism in Secularizing South Asia

The anxiety triggered by the ideology and political legacy of Vinayak Damodar Savarkar (1883–1966) centres around the ethical demands of a national state on individuals and societies in those parts of the world where the communities have not obligingly died out, and where the violence needed to create a modern nation-state does not enjoy any intrinsic legitimacy. Many sense the presence within them of the same ruthlessness and calculative cruelty that Savarkar sought to bring to the process, as inescapable parts of nation-building and state-formation; they are doubly hostile to a person who has come to personify the psychopathic tendencies that the processes of state-formation and nation-building tend to unleash and legitimize.

This essay traces the trajectory of Savarkar's life through its many vicissitudes and internal contradictions, to examine the deeper consistencies in his political beliefs and the sources of his absolute, uncritical faith in the modern state and its secular imperatives. Probably more than any other Indian leader of his time, Savarkar was in awe of Europe's achievements in the area of nation-building and state-formation. And such was the wide acceptance of these achievements in urban, middle-class India that few noticed that the basic categories of Savarkar's political ideology—nation, national state, nationality, and nationalism—always remained aggressively European. It was his misfortune that, in his lifetime, this middle class was not a sizeable part of the country and he never emerged as a popular leader with a large mass base, not even as a leader of the Hindus. That position was occupied by Mohandas Karamchand Gandhi (1869–1948), a late entrant in Indian politics, much less erudite, and full of 'strange', 'hare-brained' political ideas that, Savarkar felt, could only hobble the future of the Indian state. This essay is an effort to relocate Savarkar in the contemporary culture of Indian politics in his own terms, which also happens to be a major element in the global politics and in the emerging discourse of the Indian nation-state as it makes a bid for recognition as a future super power. After all, he is the disowned father of the new Indian nation waiting for the time when he, along with his proxy Nathuram Godse, will be restored to their rightful place among the pantheon that presides over India's fate.

ℰᴄ

However, before entering the world of Savarkar, a few comments on the context of this essay on his life. First, Savarkar is often seen as a Hindu extremist. Like everything else in this part of the world, this view has its own distinctive features. Those concerned not with academic puzzle-solving, but with live problems of religion and violence in South Asia know the anomalies that mark the public career of 'religious extremism', caught between the culture of the global nation-state system; the remnants of nineteenth-century colonial culture; and the everyday practices, values, and categories of popular religion in the region. Thus, under the umbrella of fundamentalism, there are clear differences between those who insist on total, literal allegiance to a sacred text and those who carefully avoid the issue and bypass the substantive contents of faith, to pursue the secular interests of a religious community, invoking faith as only a strategy of mobilization.

This is not a matter of personal whimsy. Political communities and movements often oscillate between the two extremes. Thus, the content of Islam for many decades was not a serious concern of Muslim nationalism in South Asia, though it has increasingly become so. Both strands are still visible in Pakistan, but it has become more difficult to admit publicly that the founder of the state, Mohammed Ali Jinnah (1876–1948), was an anti-clerical, secular, Westernized liberal in personal life, routinely breaking some of the injunctions of Islam in matters of food and drink. In Sikhs, too, there has been a similar oscillation between Sikh nationalism and fundamentalism. For a while, during the 1980s and 1990s, the latter was more visible; now it is less so.

The Hindu nationalism that has become an important player in Indian politics has mostly thrown up leaders to whom contents of faith hardly matter, even though their politics and rhetoric have changed the contours of Hinduism among some sections of Indians. It took the Rashtriya Swayamsevak Sangh (RSS), deemed the steel frame of Hindu nationalism, around fifteen years to find a serious, believing Hindu interested in theology and religious rituals to head it (and to become a target of Savarkar's private barbs for this). And only during the Ramjanmabhumi movement (1989–92) did the RSS flout its conventions to allow religious icons to enter its precincts.

Such anomalies are clues to the inner world of those who participate in or shape ethnoreligious movements and an invitation to empathetically plumb the complexities of persons involved. Yet, this has become increasingly difficult because it is now seen as either an attempt to whitewash the violence and hatred such leaders and their acolytes spew, or an insult to the religious or cultural sentiments of a community. As a result, serious cultural psychological explorations of militant nationalism as well as millennialism are becoming rarer in South Asia. In the wake of 11 September 2001, such cultivated blindness and tacit censorship are now also being indirectly endorsed by the global cultures of politics and knowledge.

Also, the early post-World War II scholars of religious and ethnic prejudice and violence—particularly those that were a response to the European genocide of the 1940s—worked in an environment in which there was inchoate, vague tiredness with cruelty, hatred, and gratuitous violence. By studying the authoritarian personality as a clinical syndrome, some of these scholars sought to universalize their work, but remained on the whole captive to the dominant culture of European modernity and heritage of the Enlightenment, both beautifully oblivious of the way massive genocidal projects had been mounted and successfully executed with impunity outside Europe over the previous 150 years, often in the name of scientific rationality and Enlightenment values.[1] Indeed, such violence was often seen as an

[1] Theodor W. Adorno, Else Frenkel-Brunswick, Daniel Levinson, R. Nevitt Sanford, *The Authoritarian Personality* (New York: Harper, 1960); see also Milton Rokeach, *The Open and Closed Mind* (New York: Basic, 1960).

ugly but unavoidable part of statecraft and justified in social evolutionary terms or as part of a new medical regime of social hygiene and eugenics. Joan Robinson, the radical economist and manifestly an opponent of colonialism, used to famously claim that the only thing worse than being colonized was not being colonized.

This is not unique to our times or to the culture that produced Savarkar. Everyone has his or her own ideas of the sanctity and meaning that must attach to some instances of megadeaths and the reasons why those responsible for such incidents should not be allowed to 'over-contextualize' their genocidal acts as products of a sick society or mind. Even the psychoanalytic tradition, which has significantly deepened our insight into contemporary Satanism, is not free of such debates. Psychoanalyst Bruno Bettelheim was convinced that fellow-psychoanalyst Robert J. Lifton's book, *Nazi Doctors*, based on intensive interviews with homicidal doctors, humanized the Nazis and, hence, was politically and ethically culpable.[2] The fear of de-demonizing an enemy with a proven record of Satanism persists. Hatred remains respectable when directed against the hateful and the 'hatable', whether the target is Osama bin Laden or George Bush.[3] The global culture of common sense leaves lesser scope for one to empathize with one's subjects, even for purposes of research.

As a result, what Philip Rieff used to call the 'analytic attitude', has often been sacrificed at the altar of political and

[2] Robert J. Lifton, *Nazi Doctors: Medical Killings and the Psychology of Genocide* (New York: Basic Books, 1986); Bruno Bettelheim, 'Their Specialty Was Murder' (Review of Robert J. Lifton's *Nazi Doctors*), *New York Times*, 5 October 1986.

[3] Contemporary statecraft, too, demands such demonization as a necessary part of executive responsibility when living with global media systems. See, for instance, a recent exploration of the issue in Peter Chambers, 'Abu Musab Al Zaraqawi: The Making and Unmaking of an American Monster (in Baghdad)', *Alternatives: Global, Local, Political*, February 2012, 37(1), pp. 30–51.

academic correctness masquerading as commitment to secular humanism and radicalism.[4] On the one hand, ethnoreligious and ultra-nationalist extremism demands a unidimensional, heroic picture of sacrifice and martyrdom; on the other, those fighting it fear that any humane treatment of the subjectivities associated with such extremism will only acknowledge the humanity of the enemy and legitimize its politics. There is the unacknowledged fear in both that the enemy may not turn out to be an alien, infra-human species, but a dangerous human potentiality within everyone; that serious psychological explorations might reveal continuities rather than unbridgeable gaps. It is not easy to say these days what Lifton once did: 'Yes, that was the Germans, that has been the Jews, but it's anyone. It's a universal potential which different groups may embrace or feel victimized by.'[5]

In recent years, the growth of religion-based violence in South Asia has spawned an array of demonologies and a rich vocabulary that eschews shades of grey. Terms such as fundamentalist, fascist, fanatic, terrorist, and Religious Right are routinely bandied, to set up what Erik Erikson used to call a new 'pseudo-species', which has to be annihilated the way the enemy would like to annihilate its targets and opponents. The vocabulary establishes a regime of indignation, disgust, and revulsion, and of censorship imposed on enquiries into human motivations and technologies of self.[6]

This essay will now make this point in a more roundabout way by entering the world of one such ideologue, to show that

---

[4] Philip Rieff, *Freud: The Mind of the Moralist* (New York: Viking, 1959).

[5] Robert J. Lifton, 'Wellfleet Conference on Historical Memory', *The Psychohistory Review*, 1986, 14(3), pp. 5–66; see p. 20.

[6] Arindam Chakrabarti, 'The Uses of Revulsion: Ethics and Aesthetics of Disgust', Plenary Lecture at the 9th East-West Philosophers' Conference, East-West Centre, Honolulu, June 2005. See also Martha Nussbaum,

what appears at first to be an unforgivable depravity could be an ideological solution that an era and a globally dominant culture of public life promoted as part of sanity and rationality. Indeed, in many Afro-Asian societies, such solutions constituted a psychological trap in colonial times; some escaped it, but most did not. Savarkar, the freedom fighter turned Muslim-baiter turned the man behind the assassination of Mohandas Karamchand Gandhi, arrived at an ethnonationalism that could only be called an illegitimate child of modern Europe, at the time routinely dumping its intellectual wares in the colonies as culture-free, universal components of secular salvation. Savarkar is an extreme case of the way an entire generation of South Asian political activists and ideologues thought. Yet, to my knowledge only one young scholar, perhaps unburdened by the intellectual baggage that earlier generations carried, has come close to saying that directly:

> For Savarkar, the sphere of politics could only be occupied by rational, secular and scientific thought.
>
> Ironically, the man who spent his life preaching the need to 'Hinduize' the political sphere detested the presence of piety/religiosity in politics. ...
>
> In Savarkar's eyes, Gandhi represented everything that was wrong with Hinduism, with its 'effeminacy' and its 'mystical' and 'irrational' approach. ... It was his life's mission to provide a counter-politics to that of Gandhi, thereby fashioning a Hinduism that stressed history, science, reason and masculinity.[7]

'Danger to Human Dignity: The Revival of Disgust and Shame in the Law', *The Chronicle of Higher Education*, 6 August 2004, http://chronicle.com/free/v50/i48/48b00601.html (accessed on 11 July 2012). I am thankful to Chakrabarti for drawing my attention to this work.

[7] Aparna Devare, *History and the Making of a Modern Hindu Self* (New Delhi: Routledge, 2011), pp. 153–5.

In the following pages, I shall disobey Clifford Geertz's injunction and supply only a thin description of the person and his times. Data on Savarkar's personal life are scarce, though some of the ongoing work on him promise to do better. His best known, full-length, serious biography is also, as its title suggests, a hagiography; it mostly shuns his private life and interpersonal relations. Even the names of his wife and children, though mentioned cursorily in the text, find no place in the index. Following the conventions of life stories in many South Asian cultures, the biographer reads Savarkar's childhood and family life strictly through the prism of adult Savarkar's political career and ideology.[8] Savarkar's own autobiographical writings are not much better; they too are, apart from being self-righteous, fearful of all human subjectivities, in an attempt to be rational, logical, secular, scientific, and modern.

જ

Sections of urban, middle-class, modernizing Hindus of British India were reborn as fragments of a pan-Indian Hindu nation only in the 1940s, roughly hundred years after the idea itself was born. This process of nation-building is not yet complete

---

[8] Dhananjay Keer, *Veer Savarkar* (Bombay: Popular Prakashan, 1950). Nevertheless, the present essay has gained much from Keer's work and the correctives to it in A.G. Noorani, *Savarkar and Hindutva: The Godse Connection* (New Delhi: LeftWord, 2002); and Suresh Sharma, 'Savarkar's Quest for a Modern Hindu Consolidation', *Studies in Humanities and Social Sciences*, 2(2), pp. 189–215. For an insightful, nuanced discussion of the cultural status of the autobiography in India and the bifurcation of the genre into *jīvanvrittānta* and *ātmakathā* by Gandhi, see Bhikhu Parekh, 'Indianization of Autobiography', in *Colonialism, Tradition and Reform: An Analysis of Gandhi's Political Discourse* (New Delhi: Sage, 1989), pp. 247–66.

and it may never be complete. However, it has gone far in urban, educated, middle- and upper-middle class India where individualism and social and occupational mobility have steadily grown since the nineteenth century. (The process has gone farthest among the Hindu diaspora in the First World. Some Hindus there have begun to think of themselves as part of a Hindu *ummah*, but that is not our concern at the moment.) Both the individuation and the mobility have taken place in a relatively impersonal, contractual, anonymous, urban-industrial context, where mainstream Hinduism in all its diversity—its innumerable castes (some figures go as high as 70,000), tens of thousands of village gods and goddesses, hundreds of sects, thousands of vernacular religious epics and *jatipuranas*, family priests, and personal and family deities, rituals, and practices specific to castes, sects, and regions—cannot be sustained.

The demand for Hinduism as a religion that an ordinary socially and geographically mobile householder—as opposed to a world renouncer—could carry within him or her as a portable device was a direct product of colonial political economy and the growth of presidency towns. At the moment of its birth, this new Hinduism—also sometimes called reformed Hinduism, proudly by some, wryly by others—did not look like Hinduism at all to a vast majority of Indians, Hindus and non-Hindus. To them, such an essentialized, desiccated Hinduism, seeking to cover so many incompatible religious practices, lifestyles, and theologies, seemed absurd.[9] This majority was to be surprised; it had

[9] Years ago, I plotted the process of this reform along two axes—Semiticization and revaluation of Kshatriya virtues—mainly to supplement the socially more critical process of Sanskritization that M.N. Srinivas has so famously studied. Ashis Nandy, *The Intimate Enemy: Loss and Recovery of Self under Colonialism* (New Delhi: Oxford University Press, 1983). The third axis

not reckoned with the new psychological demands crystallizing in colonial India.

It was a slow and painful process of birth. Among Hindus, the first well-known group to talk of the Hindus as an incipient national community was probably the Young Bengal Group in the 1840s at Calcutta, then the capital of British India. The group saw itself as a collection of reformers and talked of the Hindus and Hinduism critically, sometimes with contempt. The process was underwritten by the colonial tendency, reflected in the ruling culture of the Raj and in missionary tracts, to see Hindus as a community defined—and doomed—by their religion and the gradual institutionalization of this tendency in colonial law, education, administration, and census. Partly as a reaction, within a decade or two, the idea of the Hindus as a nation found a different status and intellectual respectability in the writings of Bhudev Mukhopadhyay (1827–1894), a social and political thinker, and Bankimchandra Chattopadhyay (1838–1894), India's first important novelist. They, too, were critical of many things Hindu but were even more critical of the Anglicized Indians who thought Hinduism could not be retooled for modern times.[10] In another two decades had emerged Brahmabandhav Upadhyay (1861–1907), a Catholic theologian and Vedantic scholar, who ran into trouble with the

---

was missing—the emergence of a generic, 'portable', tamed Hinduism that would make sense not only to scholars and theologians but also to a socially and geographically mobile householder, cut off from his or her local, vernacular roots. To survive in the contemporary world, that new Hinduism had to be more open to Hindu nationalism and more compatible with the culture of a modern nation-state.

[10] Sudipta Kaviraj, *The Unhappy Consciousness: Bankimchandra Chattopadhyay and the Formation of Nationalist Discourse in India* (New Delhi: Oxford University Press, 1995).

church in his lifetime but was to be rediscovered towards the end
of the twentieth century as a pioneer in indigenous Christian
theology. In his other incarnation, Upadhyay was a Hindu
nationalist scholar-activist and theorist of violence—so at least
it seemed to his friend Rabindranath Tagore (1861–1941).
As is well-known, Tagore's novel *Char Adhyaya* is built around
Upadhyay and Upadhyay's guilty awareness of nationalism as a
sanction for ruthless, machine violence that involved viewing
human life and human emotions instrumentally.[11] One could
argue that it was the desacralized, secular part of Upadhyay's
political Hinduism that finally ended up as Savarkar's theories
of state and nationality.[12]

The idea that the Hindus were the carriers of an overly diverse
religion called Hinduism by default—and, to that extent, were an
ill-formed, sleep-walking crypto-nation that had not actualized
its possibilities—was to later become a central assumption
of Hindu nationalism. Naturally, a certain admiration for Christianity and Islam, as religions in better touch with the processes
of state-formation and nation-building, was the obverse of such
nationalism. All Hindu reform movements borrowed from these

---

[11] Upadhyay in many respects served as Tagore's double. All three explicitly political novels of Tagore—*Gora* (1909), *Ghare Baire* (1916), and *Char
Adhyaya* (1934)—negotiate the personality and ideology of Upadhyay. For a
while in his youth, Tagore himself was close to Hindu nationalism and, when
he was moving out of that phase, he found Upadhyay moving towards his abandoned ideology. Ashis Nandy, *The Illegitimacy of Nationalism: Rabindranath
Tagore and the Politics of Self* (New Delhi: Oxford University Press, 1989).

[12] Ibid. For a detailed and insightful look at Upadhyay, see Julius Lipner, *Life
and Thought of a Revolutionary* (New Delhi: Oxford University Press, 1999).
Others elsewhere in India were moving towards Upadhyay's position, indicat-
ing that it was something more than an idiosyncratic, personal choice. Only
a few years later, Har Dayal (1888–1939) in north India began articulating
a similar idea of political Hinduism, though without an explicit theory of
violence.

two faiths to correct the 'inadequacies' of Hinduism. Such a stance was then popular among the modernizing middle-class, which endorsed the contempt and hostility that often tinged Hindu nationalist attitudes towards the Hindus. The overdone emphases on Hindu pride and masculinization of the Hindus was built on such self-hatred.

Vinayak Damodar Savarkar in 1923 reinvented a term previously used by the likes of Brahmabandhav Upadhyay to describe this ideology: Hindutva.[13] Hindutva, Savarkar made clear, was not the same as Hinduism, despite what an unthinking Indian Supreme Court was to declare eighty years later.[14] Hindutva was a form of political Hinduism that sought to organize and militarize the Hindus as a nationality. Without such nationality, the argument went, there could be no basis for nationalism in a highly diverse society, and without nationalism there could be no nation-state. From the beginning, Hindutva had a strong masculine content. Savarkar was probably the first and the last to call India a fatherland (*pitrubhu*) and not a motherland (*matrubhumi*). To introduce this continental usage, he had to dredge Sanskrit grammar to shed the common term *bhumi* (land), which was feminine, and use the rarer *bhu*. For this pitrubhu you could not even sing one of the unofficial national anthem of the freedom fighters, *Vande Mataram*, a paean to Mother India.

---

[13] Vinayak Damodar Savarkar, *Hindutva: Who is a Hindu?* (1923) (Bombay: Veer Savarkar, 1969).

[14] Justice J.S. Verma, who delivered the judgement, was to, however, later claim that politicians had misused his judgement, without admitting that the judgement gave a suspect political ideology the status of a religion, which even Savarkar and the RSS had not claimed or done. On Justice Verma's self-justification, see 'My Verdict was Misinterpreted', *Hindustan Times*, 7 February 2003.

To this fatherland, Savarkar believed, the Hindus had an exclusive right by virtue of the sacred geography associated with it. Amnon Raz-Krakotzkin defines the secular Zionist as the one who believes that there is no God but insists that He has given the land of Israel to the Jews nonetheless.[15] Savarkar, a hard-boiled atheist who did not believe in sacred geographies, was even less embarrassed to claim the whole of India for the Hindus on the grounds of sacred geography.

When Savarkar propounded his two-nation theory—the first to explicitly do so in South Asia—it was a clear sixteen years before the Muslim League embraced the idea of the Hindus and the Muslims as two distinctive nations and demanded the division of India. His pioneering efforts in this respect were recognized. Historian R.C. Majumdar, who called Savarkar a 'great revolutionary leader', was clear about wherefrom the League got its inspiration: it 'took serious notice of the frank speeches of Savarkar.'[16] But the idea of nationhood as the marker of a people was not Savarkar's either; he borrowed it from European thinkers like Guiseppe Mazzini (1805–1872). Mazzini was not unknown in India, thanks to the early Bengali Hindu nationalists such as Upadhyay. Only the likes of Upadhyay did not include in their repertoire an ideology of political and cultural exclusion, leavened with hatred, as Savarkar was to do. In a public speech in 1925, Savarkar said that Indians had to learn to eschew soft values like 'humility, self-surrender and forgiveness' and

[15] Amnon Raz-Krakotzkin, presentation in the session on 'Contemporary Debates in the West: Secular Norms, Multiculturalism, and Immigrant Incorporation', conference on 'The Secular, Secularizations, and Secularisms' at the Wissenschaftskolleg, Berlin, 7–10 June 2006.
[16] R.C. Majumdar quoted in A.G. Noorani, *Savarkar and Hindutva: The Godse Connection* (New Delhi: LeftWord, 2002).

cultivate 'sturdy habits of hatred, retaliation, vindictiveness'.[17] Occasionally he went further. At one place in his writings, he seems miserable that his heroes, Shivaji and Chinaji Appa, did not rape Muslim women, 'because of then prevalent suicidal ideas about chivalry to women, which ultimately proved highly detrimental to the Hindu community.'[18]

To spite admirers who might think this to be an aberration, in 1965 at the age of 82, Savarkar wrote in the wake of the India–Pakistan war that took place that year: 'Pakistan's barbaric acts such as kidnapping and raping Indian women would not be stopped unless Pakistan was given tit for tat.' One suspects that violence to Savarkar was not merely a revolutionary tool, but an end in itself, as if he was seeking legitimate targets to express the free-floating rage within him.[19] This rage coloured not only his ruthlessness but also the touch of maudlin romance in it. He was a very cruel man, a relative once confided to a fellow researcher.

---

[17] M.R. Jayakar, *Story of My Life*, Vol. 2, p. 541, quoted in Noorani, *Savarkar and Hindutva*, pp. 25–6.

[18] V.D. *Savarkar, The Six Golden Epochs of Indian History* (New Delhi: Rajdhani Granthanagar, 1970), p. 71. Quoted by Kavita Krishnan, 'Unveiling Savarkar: Imperfect', www. Cpiml.org/liberation/year-2003/April. For a detailed, well-researched discussion of Savarkar on rape and his belief that a woman's body can be a political instrument and weapon and the Hindus must learn to use this weapon, see Purushottam Agarwal, 'Savarkar, Surat and Draupadi: Legitimising Rape as a Political Weapon', in Tanika Sarkar and Urvashi Butalia (eds), *A Review of Women and the Hindu Right* (New Delhi: Kali for Women, 1996), pp. 29–57.

[19] Even this may not be the whole story. Lloyd deMause has argued that the origins of war lie partly in the fantasy of war as righteous rape. Savarkar might have reversed the process, imagining rape as a form of war that allegedly makes nations. Lloyd deMause, *The Emotional Life of Nations* (New York: Karnac Books, 2002), Ch. 6. Suresh Sharma argues that Savarkar reneged on the inclusive nationalism of his earlier years 'not because Hindu rashtra represented a

Savarkar may not have been straightforward about many things, but he had a Brahminic respect for ideas. When in the 1940s Mohammed Ali Jinnah began to go places with his two-nation theory, Savarkar was honest enough to say: 'I have no quarrel with Mr Jinnah's two-nation theory. We Hindus are a nation by ourselves and it is a historical fact that Hindus and Muslims are two nations.'[20]

ೞ

At this point let me quickly outline Savarkar's life. Vinayak Damodar Savarkar was born in a Chitpavan Brahmin family in a village near Nasik in 1883.[21] It was a landed family that was also into money-lending. However, his father Damodarpant was known more for his poetry and his knowledge of Sanskrit and Western classics than for his land holdings. Vinayak was the second son of his parents. His two brothers were also to become freedom fighters and one of them was to be sentenced to life imprisonment at Andamans. He also had a younger sister. The family goddess of

higher ideal' but because he came to the conclusion that his earlier project was not a feasible one, whereas a Hindu nation was a realizable goal. Sharma, 'Savarkar's Quest', p. 202. Sharma is not wrong but his interpretation does not fully explain the low rhetoric and passions of an otherwise Machiavellian politician who was proudly dispassionate and impersonal. For that one must take into account the inner demons that populated Savarkar's world.

[20] *Indian Annual Register*, 1943, Vol. 2, p. 10. Quoted in Anil Nauriya, 'The Savarkarist Syntax', *The Hindu*, 18 September 2004.

[21] On the political-cultural context from within which Savarkar emerged and within which he made sense, see Enrico Fasana, 'Deshabhakta: The Leaders of the Indian Independence Movement in the Eyes of Marathi Nationalists', *Asian and African Studies*, 1994, 3(2), pp. 152–75; and 'From Hindutva to Hindu Rashtra: The Social and the Political Thought of Vinayak Damodar Savarkar (1883–1966)', presented at the 13th European Conference on Modern South Asian Studies, Toulouse, 31 August–3 September 1996.

the Savarkars was Bhavani and one biographer identifies her as a local goddess. Perhaps she was. But she had other connections, too. She was the personal goddess of Shivaji and was an important deity of revolutionaries of Bengal. 'Jai Bhavani' was also the war cry of Guru Govind Singh who turned the Sikhs into a martial community.

Biographies suggest a Hindu nationalist atmosphere at young Savarkar's home, but that was not rare then in educated Chitpavan households. One of the few Brahmin communities to have tasted real political power in the declining years of the Mughal Empire, Chitpavans were highly successful in the professions under the Raj but seemed to resent their loss of power. Part of the resentment against the British, Aparna Devare feels, was displaced on to Muslims.[22] Perhaps more significant were the vague indications of an amoral, violent streak in young Vinayak. Keer tells how Vinayak, as a child, proudly vandalized a local mosque with his friends and, then, had a brawl with angry Muslim boys.[23]

From his early years Vinayak was a voracious reader and had superb memory. His poetry was first published when he was ten. This might have been a response to the sudden death of his mother from cholera the same year. Vinayak was particularly fond of his mother and she had been his refuge from a stern, disciplinarian father, not averse to occasionally meting out heavy doses of physical punishment.[24] Her death must have been traumatizing. One wonders if the maudlin nationalism of his early years, so clearly associated with his deification of Mother India on the one hand, and his deep faith in goddess Bhavani on the other, had something to do with Savarkar's emotional closeness

[22] Devare, *History and the Making of a Modern Hindu Self*, p. 158.
[23] Keer, *Veer Savarkar*, pp. 4–5. This is the only instance of Muslims entering the life of young Savarkar, Devare says. Devare, Ibid.
[24] Ibid., Ch. 1.

to his own mother. For, later, when he lost his faith and turned an abrasive rationalist and political realist, he tried hard to disown this part of himself and to masculinize the entire mythic substratum of his nationalism. As we have seen, he ended up reconceptualizing India as a fatherland.

Vinayak also turned out to be a good public speaker; at the age of 14, he won a prize for elocution. At around the same time, deeply moved by the hanging of the Chapekar brothers by the British regime, he took a vow at the altar of his family goddess, Bhavani, to fight for India's freedom. He even started in 1899, as a 16-year-old student, an anti-imperialist Friends' Circle, Mitra Mela. The same year his father and uncle died of plague. His two brothers also contacted the disease but recovered. Vinayak's elder brother, Babarao, had to now bear the burden of maintaining the family. Life for the three brothers had suddenly become unpredictable and cruel; there were reasons for them to be bitter with fate and its treacherous ways.

After matriculating from the city of Nasik in 1901, Vinayak joined Fergusson College at Poona (now Pune) in 1902, where he quickly gave up his traditional Indian dress and took to European dress, which he had always wanted to wear. Though he duly completed his studies and passed his examination, his degree was withheld because of his political activities. Fortunately, he won a scholarship to go to England in 1906. There, at the age of 23, he established another anti-imperialist group called Free India Society. They produced a manual on bomb-making and sent copies of it to India and Savarkar himself produced a Marathi translation of Mazzini's writings, which was published from India.

In 1908, to commemorate the 50th anniversary of the rebellion of 1857 against British rule, the Sepoy Mutiny, Savarkar published his well-known tract, *The First Indian War of Independence—1857*, which many consider to be his best work.

A.G. Noorani, no admirer of Savarkar, calls it a 'veritable classic'.[25] The government dutifully proscribed it but it was republished from Holland. Savarkar also led the Indian students in celebrating martyr's day on the 50th anniversary of the 1857 uprising. He was then not even 25. In 1909, he heard in England that his brother had been sentenced to transportation for life at Andaman for his revolutionary activities. Soon afterwards, Madanlal Dhingra, his one-time colleague and protégé, was caught after he killed a colonial bureaucrat at London at Savarkar's instigation.[26]

Savarkar met Mohandas Karamchand Gandhi for the first time at London. Much of Savarkar's life was to be later defined by his differences with and antipathy towards Gandhi. He had contempt for Gandhi's 'unscientific' and 'unscholarly' mind, and he despised Gandhi's critique of the urban-industrial vision and modern technology and preoccupation with things like truth force, fasting, and concern for the cow.[27] Above all, as an obedient student of Europe's political history, he hated Gandhi's non-violence, which Savarkar thought irreconcilable with modern—and, of course, European—politics and statecraft. 'Absolute non-violence,' he would later declare, was 'absolutely sinful.' Later, he came to develop as strong a dislike for the charkha or spinning wheel and Gandhi's pacifist interpretation of the Gita. They all seemed to Savarkar forms of primitivism, gloriously ignorant of what modern science and political theory

---

[25] It is a remarkable coincidence that Savarkar's book was published more or less at the same time as Gandhi's *Hind Swaraj*, which projected an entirely different view of India's self-definition and political future, and Rabindranath Tagore's novel *Gora*, a sophisticated rebuttal of Savarkar's ideology from a prescient, proto-Gandhian point of view.

[26] S.S. Savarkar and G.M. Joshi (eds), *Historical Statements by V.D. Savarkar* (Bombay: Popular Prakashan, 1967), p. 114.

[27] Keer, *Veer Savarkar*, p. 530.

had to offer India. It is said that when Gandhi once came to meet him at London at India House, Savarkar was cooking prawns, his favourite. When Gandhi broached some issue, Savarkar cut him short, 'we can discuss it later ... first come and have your food with us.' When Gandhi said he was a vegetarian, Savarkar reportedly retorted, 'If you cannot eat with us, how on earth are you going to work with us.' Incidentally, Savarkar, born a vegetarian, ate meat even though he did not like its taste, because he associated meat-eating with virility and masculinity.[28] His contempt for the effeminate, retrogressive, vegetarian Gujarati Bania never subsided.[29]

This story is symptomatic of a basic personality difference between the two persons and their rival ideologies of freedom. The four years of Savarkar's exposure to the West at the prime of his youth, as his doting biographer Harindra Srivastava recognizes, had remade him as a secular, modern, Western-educated Indian who had studied mainstream British life, literature, culture, and British mind.[30] Mazzini was already his God and he suffered

[28] Devare, History and the Making of a Modern Hindu Self, p. 157.
[29] Harindra Srivastava, Five Stormy Years: Savarkar in London (New Delhi: Allied, 1983), pp. 28–9. As for the meal Savarkar and Gandhi shared, there are a number of versions; I have used only one of them. In any case, one result of the meeting was that, when Gandhi next visited India House in 1909 to preside over Dussehra celebrations, he made it a condition that only vegetarian food will be served. On the basic philosophical clash between Savarkar's modernism, including his total commitment to modern science and technology, and Gandhi's radical, futuristic critique of modernity, the urban-industrial vision and Baconian science and technology, see Suresh Sharma, 'Savarkar's Quest'; A. Raghuramaraju, Debates in Indian Philosophy: Classical, Colonial, and Contemporary (New Delhi: Oxford University Press, 2006), pp. 66–91; and Ashis Nandy, 'From Outside the Imperium: Gandhi's Cultural Critique of the West', in Traditions, Tyranny and Utopias: Essays in the Politics of Awareness (New Delhi: Oxford University Press, 1987), pp. 127–63.
[30] Srivastava, Five Stormy Years, p. 4.

from what some biographers have called a 'Mazzinimania';[31] his stay in England now equipped him with European concepts and methods of statecraft and protest. Gandhi, on the other hand, had cussedly chosen to decide which West would influence him and how much; he searched for and discovered another West that could be an ally of not only his political but also cultural self. He refused to be retooled as a standardized, progressive nationalist or as a conventional revolutionary.[32]

In due course, Savarkar qualified as a barrister from Grey's Inn, but he refused to give an undertaking that he would not participate in seditious activities and was not called to the bar. (As we shall see, that might have been the last time Savarkar refused to give an undertaking under pressure from authorities.) Such incidences of dissidence and his earlier secret revolutionary activities had a cumulative effect. In 1910, he was arrested and deported to India. On the way to India, he tried to escape at Marseilles but was recaptured, even though it was French territory. Presumably, even post-revolutionary, republican France, when it came to anti-colonial violence, knew where and when to draw a line, so far as its ideas of freedom and sovereignty went.

Savarkar was tried in India and was sentenced to transportation for life twice over, which meant jail for fifty years. His property, too, was confiscated.[33] The university cancelled his

[31] Ibid., p. 33; also see S.L. Karandikar, *Savarkar Charitra* (Pune: Modern Book Depot, 1947), p. 33.

[32] For Savarkar's version of his days in England, see *Inside the Enemy Camp*, www.savarkar.org

[33] The property was not returned to him in independent India either. When the last request in Savarkar's life time was made to Morarji Desai, then Chief Minister of Bombay, Desai was unambiguous. He said that the harm Savarkar had done to the country in his later life outweighed the good he did to it earlier. Keer, *Veer Savarkar*, p. 406.

BA degree. At the age of 27, Savarkar was sent to the notorious Cellular Jail at Port Blair in Andaman Islands.

The journey to Port Blair was itself traumatic. He was to later write:

> Climbing into the steamer to be transported for life was like putting a live man in his own coffin. Hundreds and thousands must have gone to the Andamans ... and not ten in a thousand had returned alive to India! Young men of 18, as soon as they put their step on the steamer, became old and the shadow of death was visible on their faces.[34]

The Cellular Jail, Savarkar soon found out, took its notoriety seriously and tried to live up to its image the hard way. The jail's walls were adorned with manacles and other items of torture and sadism was a part of everyday life.[35] He was allowed one letter a year and had to wear a plaque which said that he was sentenced in 1911 and would be released in 1960. His punishments included solitary confinement for six months, seven days of standing handcuffs, and ten days of cross bar fetters, which did not allow him to bend his knees for ten days. He was also yoked to oil like a bullock—along with two other revolutionaries, Indu Bhushan

---

[34] V.D. Savarkar, quoted in M.V. Kamath, 'Savarkar: The Limits of Human Endurance', in Verinder Grover, *V.D. Savarkar* (New Delhi: Deep and Deep, 1993), pp. 444–51; see esp. p. 445.

[35] To get a flavour of the sadomasochistic environment of Cellular Jail, as it was experienced by Savarkar, see Damodar Vinayak Savarkar, *My Transportation for Life*, tr. V.N. Naik (Bombay: Veer Savarkar Prakashan, 1984). This is a translation of the book *Mazi Janmathep* serialized in two Marathi journals during 1925–7 and later published as a book by Savarkar. For those who might be tempted to read the account as exaggerated and self-serving, there is also the more recent invocation of the concentration-camp-like ambience of the jail by two British journalists in Cathy Scott-Clark and Adrian Levy, 'Survivors of Our Hell', *Guardian Unlimited*, 23 June 2001, http://www.guardian.co.uk/Archive/Article/0,4273,4207876,00.html (accessed on 31 August 2015). Scott-Clark and Levy depend not only on survivors' testimony but also on official records. See also S.N. Aggarwal, *Heroes of Cellular Jail* (New Delhi: Rupa, 2006).

Roy and Ullaskar Dutt—to produce 30 lbs of mustard oil. (Roy committed suicide, unable to bear the torture and the humiliation, and Dutt went mad and was put in an asylum in Andamans for fourteen years.) However, what the finicky Brahmin hated most were the filthy, primitive, grossly inadequate toilet facilities. As prisoners were locked up and not allowed to use the jail toilets for about twelve hours at night, many eased themselves in their cells and had to learn to sleep next to their faeces and puddles of urine.

All this, but particularly the solitary confinement, began to induce subtle but decisive changes in the personality and world-view of Savarkar, still a young man who could hope to return home only as an old man. 'He often felt that his mind had been on a rack all the time, his nerves completely shattered.'[36] And the hardened revolutionary began to show signs of physical fright and psychological collapse. The culture of violence, cruelty, and totalism in the jail was a constant invitation to suicide and madness. One could survive that extreme situation only by radically retooling oneself to ensure survival and the costs of that retooling could be distasteful, both for the victim and the onlookers.[37]

---

[36] Kamath, 'Savarkar', p. 445.

[37] Some amount of doublespeak, ingratiation, and manipulative behaviour was common in the sick environment of Andamans, both among the prison staff and the prisoners, including some of the most respected freedom fighters. These had become inevitable tools of survival, even resistance. See Savarkar, My Transportation for Life, Ch. 16. However, Savarkar's attempts to cast himself in a heroic mould and judge others by impossible standards by which he himself could not live, did not make him particularly popular among other freedom fighters in the jail. Ideologically, he could not accept in freedom fighters the normal 'weaknesses' of human beings. He was not sensitive to the inner life of persons and his ideology had little space for human subjectivities, which he tended to see as emasculating. One revealing instance was his inability to see through the weak, fearful, insecure, scheming David Barrie, the Irish jailor who at one level was a tyrant and a sadist, and at another, a self-hating colonial

Savarkar's ideological self always had two axes: along one he worshipped modern scientific rationality and Machiavellianism, along the other he used European romanticism to empower his ideas of nationalism and revolution. His ethics probably came from the latter. The Cellular Jail crippled the romanticism, so that it now survived mainly as a rhetoric that allowed him to give fuller play to his amoral, reason-driven Machiavellian self as a technology of survival. Contrary to the impression he gives in his autobiographical writings, within a year of his arrival at Andamans he began to write abject appeals to the authorities, seeking clemency and promising loyalty, obedience, and good behaviour. There had been a manipulative streak even in his revolutionary career and he now began to take even greater care not to antagonize the jail authorities. There is at least one other respected revolutionary, Trailokya Nath Maharaj, a fellow-prisoner of Savarkar in Andamans, who complained to historian R.C. Majumdar that the Savarkar brothers egged on the political prisoners to call a strike and then did not join it.[38] Rumours say that Savarkar's experiences in jail sharpened his antipathy towards the Muslims, for the torturers included Muslim warders, two of whom allegedly sodomized him. Savarkar does mention that the warders for political prisoners in Cellular Jail were all Muslims and they were nasty.[39]

---

subject trying to ingratiate him by talking to Savarkar about his early hatred of the English and the unpleasant duties his job imposed on him. Savarkar's attempts to score debating points whenever Barrie opened a conversation with him quickened Barrie's feelings of inferiority and his lurking awareness of his moral degradation and made him doubly dangerous.

[38] R.C. Majumdar cited in Noorani, *Savarkar and Hindutva*, pp. 58–9.

[39] These rumours probably induced two popular writers to suspect that there was homosexual bonding between V.D. Savarkar and Nathuram Godse. Larry Collins and Dominique Lapiere, *Freedom at Midnight* (1975) (New York: HarperCollins, 1997). Could it be that in the masculinized worldview of

However, Savarkar's own account forces one to ask if his sufferings in the hands of his Muslim warders were not, at least partly, a result of his self-fulfilling, anti-Muslim prejudices. For instance, once an infamous, low-level functionary of the jail, a Pathan called Mirza Khan, came to Savarkar and complimented him for the loyalty, courage, and determination of Nani Gopal, a political prisoner who had gone on hunger strike and was nearing death. Khan called Gopal a 'true disciple' of Savarkar and 'verily a Pathan lad'. Savarkar's response to this attempt to establish a relationship was,

> Bada Jamadar, you are wrong. Your father was a Pathan and you are a Pathan. If he [Nani Gopal] were a Pathan, he would not have rotten in this jail for the sake of his country; he would have, like you, licked the shoes of Mr. Barrie and would not have defied him. ... It is because Nani Gopal is a born Hindu that he is so brave.[40]

That Savarkar shared the widespread stereotype of the Pathans and considered the Pathan warders to be 'ignorant blockheads'— apart from being, like the Sindhi and Baluchi Muslims, 'cruel', 'unscrupulous', 'bigoted', and 'fanatics'—did not help matters.[41] At one place in his jail memoirs, he mentions that there were exceptions among the Muslims, but his narrative has no place for any of these exceptions and his ideology does not allow him to talk of them.[42]

Hindu nationalism, these rumours, even if untrue, were a metaphoric means of recognizing the emasculation of Savarkar?

[40] Savarkar, *My Transportation for Life*, pp. 91–2, 254.

[41] Ibid., pp. 252–3.

[42] Things were seemingly different before Savarkar went to Andamans. On the way to Andamans, when he was staying in a jail at Bombay, he was helped by one of his Muslim warders and he openly acknowledged that. Before that, at London too, he had Muslim friends. Y.D. Phadke, *Shodh Savarkarancha* (Pune: Sri Vidya, 2000), p. 70, quoted in Devare, *History and the Making of a Modern Hindu Self*, p. 159.

Savarkar's admirers claim that the mercy petitions and the undertakings he signed so readily were strategic; he wanted to be released to participate in the freedom movement. It is true that the British never fully trusted his petitions and his relationship with the colonial regime did not automatically become cosy immediately afterwards, as some of his detractors insinuate. It is also true that some degree of manipulative cunning was part of Savarkar's repertoire. Filing of such petitions by political prisoners, too, was not rare. But it is also true that the authorities trusted him enough to appoint him a foreman in the jail and Savarkar never again played any significant or insignificant part in the anti-imperialist struggle. On the contrary, he openly began to look upon the British Empire as a boon and an opportunity to cleanse India of the Muslims, his version of the 'yellow peril'.[43] There was in his new politics identifiable strains of what some clinicians will diagnose as authoritarian submission and identification with his tormentors.

Savarkar's petitions paid dividends; the colonial authorities probably had a more rounded understanding of his personality than his Indian admirers and detractors. He was considered

---

[43] See G.N.S. Raghavan, 'In Search of the Real Savarkar', *Indian Express*, 8 July 2003. Raghavan tries hard to sell the colonial regime's natural suspicion of Savarkar's motives behind his mercy petitions as a proof of Savarkar's persistent faith in his political tactics. Actually, such proof is not necessary. His participation in Gandhi's murder is more than adequate proof that his tactics did not change over a period of four decades. The question is: was he willing to or psychologically capable of taking on the colonial state or, for that matter, any state after his experiences in Andamans? Savarkar was an incurable statist, but the Cellular Jail taught him a thing or two about the power and ruthlessness of states. The tone of his mercy petition to the government sent from the Cellular Jail says it all. Not only did he promise to 'serve the government in any capacity' it wanted, he also added, '... the mighty alone can afford to be merciful and therefore where else can the prodigal son return but to the parental doors of the government.' Noorani, *Savarkar and Hindutva*, p. 18.

harmless and released in 1921 at the age of 38. But the authorities did not take any chance either. After his return from Andaman in 1921, he was kept in Ratnagiri Jail for three years. The ghosts of Andamans still haunted him and this new sentence was probably the last straw. At least at one point he was depressed enough to think of suicide:

> High up in that cell was a barred window as in the jail in the Andamans. I thought out in my mind how to reach my hand to the window and how to put an end to my life by hanging myself by a rope to its bars ... my mind was overcast with complete darkness.[44]

In 1924 Savarkar was finally released on the condition that he would not participate in politics and not go outside Ratnagiri district. Indeed, 'seeing his spirit broken and willpower completely shattered', the government also suggested that he should state that his trial was fair and the sentence awarded was just. At the same time, it told him this was 'in no way ... a condition of his release'. Yet, he went ahead and made the statement.[45] The colonial system was more efficient than it itself thought; Savarkar had returned from Andamans a shadow of his old self and the three

[44] V.D. Savarkar quoted in Kamath, 'Savarkar', p. 445. Ideologically, Savarkar was against suicide, but the idea did come fleetingly to him even at Andamans. When Indu Bhushan Roy committed suicide unable to bear the life at Andamans, Savarkar said to himself, according to his own admission, 'Who knows, one day your fate will be the same as his.' Savarkar, *My Transportation for Life*, p. 216.
[45] Savarkar wrote: 'I hereby acknowledge that I had a fair trial and just sentence. I heartily abhor methods of violence resorted to in days gone by, and I feel myself duty bound to uphold Law and the constitution to the best of my powers and am willing to make the Reform [Montagu-Chelmsford proposals of 1919, rejected by virtually every Indian political party] a success in so far as I may be allowed to do so in future.' Krishnan Dubey and Venkitesh Ramakrishnan, 'Far from Heroism—The Tale of "Veer Savarkar" and a Response', *Frontline*, 7 April 1996, http://www.frontline.in/the-nation/savarkar-and-gandhi/articles6805181.ece#VePkihXnhik.mailto (accessed on 31 August 2015).

additional years in jail, too, had done their job. When released in 1924, 'at forty one he looked sixty and resembled a lean and hungry hawk, with bitter mouth and eyes that looked hooded.'[46]

It was in Ratnagiri Jail that Savarkar wrote the tract, *Hindutva* (1923), which still serves as the Bible of Hindu nationalists.[47] Savarkar had started public life as a secular, reasonably non-sectarian, anti-imperialist activist. He might have already been a bit of a Hindu chauvinist but that did not distort much of his political ideas. One indicator is his book on 1857. Even his favourite argument that the holy land, *punyabhu*, for Muslims and Christians was outside India—and hence they could not be equal partners in a common nationality—does not find a place in the book.[48] *Hindutva* was the milestone in a journey that was to devour him. There are hints in the book of a totalism that induced him to marry even his classical scholarship to concerns that had little to do with classicism and everything to with imperial Europe and with categories that had already become the core concern of an imperial knowledge system—nationality, national culture,

[46] Robert Payne, *The Life and Death of Mahatma Gandhi* (London: Bodley Head, 1968), p. 208.

[47] When Madhavrao Sadashiv Golwalkar (1906–1973), the head of the RSS during 1940–73, attempted an updated handbook on Hindu nationalism, he ended up crudely parroting Savarkar, even though he had been a butt of Savarkar's biting sarcasm for his softness towards Hindu rituals and beliefs. See M.S. Golwalkar, *We or Our Nationhood Defined* (Nagpur: Bharat Prakashan, 1939). Golwalkar reportedly showed the manuscript of the book to one of Savarkar's brothers for comments, criticisms, and suggestions. It did not help, for Savarkar's aim was to produce nothing less than a house-broken, defanged version of Hinduism that would be subservient to a modern nation-state.

[48] It is surprising that to a person as obsequiously and uncritically European in his political thought as Savarkar, it never occurred that every European nationality had its holy land not only outside their country but outside Europe as well. Probably he thought that Europe was advanced and modern enough to have outgrown its ethnoreligious past and denominational differences, and could sustain its nationalities on rational and secular grounds alone.

nation-building state-formation, secular rationality, and a social-evolutionary concept of history. Each of these imported ideas were absolutized, seen as sacrosanct and all traditions, however sacred, were expected to be subservient to it.

In politics, if you wear a mask long enough, it becomes your face. Savarkar's peculiar mix of collaboration and xenophobia gradually devoured him, though it also perhaps helped to hold together his post-Andaman self. Politics had always given him the scope to publicly express his more psychopathic and violent traits, and he was learned enough to know that modern nation-building and state-formation had been a violent, criminal enterprise in almost all societies. At the same time, being a typical product of late nineteenth-century colonial knowledge system, he could think of India only as a potential, European-style nation-state. Once he had thought through this issue, his authoritarian traits did not permit him any ambiguity in this matter. The 'prince of revolutionaries' now openly redefined British colonial rule as an apprenticeship, which taught the Indians the principles of 'normal' nationhood. He was too deeply seeped in history, the new obsession of India's modern elite,[49] not to notice that the basis of nation- and state-building in each and every European country had been, to start with, religion and ethnicity. He was one of those who had not only taken to heart the 'lessons' of Europe's political history, but also wanted all Indians to live by that history.[50]

---

[49] Kaviraj, *Unhappy Consciousness*, p. 109. By Indians, Kaviraj of course means the small, modernizing, urban, Brahminic middle-class India that dominated public discourse at the time.

[50] As he put it in a speech unearthed by historian Prabha Dixit (Hindu Mahasabha Records, File 13, quoted in Noorani, *Savarkar and Hindutva*, p. 34), 'in Hindustan it is the Hindus professing Hindu religion and being in overwhelming majority that constitute the national community and create and formulate the nationalism of the nation. It is so in every country of the world.'

Whether Savarkar himself fully shared the passions and symbols on which the Hindu nation was to be built is, however, another issue. Realpolitik, too, was a part of his ideological kit-bag and under his leadership his party, the Hindu Mahasabha, often collaborated and formed governments in alliance with parties that others did not expect him to touch (with the Muslim League, for instance, when the League was demanding the division of India). This manipulative use of religion and culture could not but boomerang; in Savarkar's later years it looked as if he himself had turned into the soulless instrument that he wanted the Hindus to be.

In 1937 Savarkar became the President of the Hindu Mahasabha. This was not surprising; the party was his in any case. More important was the publication of his novel *Kalapani* the same year. Savarkar was already the author of a novel, *Mopla* (1924), and a play, *Ushap* (1927). Both mirrored his ideology. *Kalapani* was something more—it reflected his and perhaps Hindutva's only attempt to envision an ideal or desirable India. He had written in 1907 *The First Indian War of Independence—1857*, which projected the idea of a unified Indian resistance to colonialism, cutting across all socio-religious barriers. At the centre of the new work, shaped by his days in Andamans, was an imaginary, futuristic, post-penal colony as the epitome of a postcolonial society. It was the vision of a secular, egalitarian, homogeneous, Hindu community where people married across linguistic and caste boundaries and shared the same culture, language, and ideology—a terribly insipid, deadly version of a fully modern nation-state with all its unmanageable angularities ironed out. *The First Indian War* was evidently a distant memory now.

Magnanimously, *Kalapani* confined its thought experiment to the Hindus. They were the ones who were to be thus homogenized for the sake of a viable national state and cured of the

Hinduism that a chaotic, amorphous Indian society had thought-lessly inculcated in the 'slumbering' Hindus over the centuries.[51] Unfortunately, though Savarkar exiles Muslims and Christians from his utopia, they are there in his novel in full strength. They haunt Savarkar's utopia as monolithic ghost communities, as fully formed nations running full-fledged states. They are there in the novel as the unacknowledged future of the Hindus.[52] *Kalapani* represents the hope of the author that, despite rebuffing him and his party, the Hindus would someday be rational enough to gulp the heavy dose of uniformity he was prescribing, for the sake of *his* idea of India.

The Hindus proved to be more headstrong; Savarkar's ideo-logy and politics only further distanced him from the freedom movement. Once World War II started in 1939, the gap widened because he began helping the colonial regime to recruit Indians as soldiers. He argued that this was his way of militarizing the Hindus. By the end of the war, he was even more of a lonely fig-ure, excluded from virtually all serious negotiations on transfer of power and the division of British India into two nation-states.

[51] As he once said in a maudlin homage to the martyrs of 1857: 'And then, oh Martyrs, tell us the little as well as the great defects which you found out in our people in that experiment of yours. But above all, point out that ruinous, nay, the only material drawback in the body of the nation which rendered all your efforts futile—the mean selfish blindness which refuses to see its way to join the nation's cause. Say that the only cause of the defeat of Hindusthan was Hin-dusthan herself.' V.D. Savarkar, *Echoes from Andamans* (Bombay: Veer Savarkar Prakashan, 1984), pp. 53–6; see pp. 55–6.

[52] Though he never directly wrote on the subject, Savarkar had swallowed hook, line, and sinker European social evolutionism. He did not approve of the Indians writing on Vedanta. He would have them write rather on politi-cal history, science, economy, and other such subjects, because, he said, 'The Americans need Vedanta and so does England; for they have developed their life to that fullness, richness and manliness—to Kshatriyahood and so stand on the threshold of that Brahminhood. But ... we are ... at present all Shudras and cannot claim access to the Veda and Vedanta.' Ibid., p. 5.

Savarkar must have been hurt that though Gandhi had helped a recruitment drive in South Africa many years ago, it was never held against Gandhi, while his recruitment drive for the British-Indian army, in a war that enjoyed much more legitimacy among the liberals and the Left, further isolated him.

Though it was Savarkar's two-nation theory that triumphed at the end and justified the partitioning of India, he was deeply distressed by the division and held Gandhi primarily responsible for it. Savarkar was never terribly self-exploratory and anti-intraception was almost an article of faith with him; like many revolutionaries he feared looking within, perhaps because he thought it would soften his resolve. In 1947 the aging rebel got involved in a plot to kill Gandhi who was threatening to become a long-term liability for the young Indian nation-state. This time Savarkar found his willing instruments in Nathuram Vinayak Godse and Narayan Apte, two of his young admirers. They were members of the Hindu Mahasabha and former members of the RSS. Godse was the one to pull the trigger on an unarmed, unprotected Gandhi on 30 January 1948.

The police and the government could have easily prevented the killing, for one of the plotters, Madanlal Pahwa, had thrown a bomb at one of Gandhi's prayer meetings a few days earlier, was caught, and within a few hours revealed all the relevant details and names of the persons involved in the plot. However, many in the ruling circles were fed up with Gandhi's 'eccentric', 'effeminate', 'irrational' defiance of the canons of modern statecraft, his non-violence, and what some Indian intellectuals had already begun to call 'pulpit politics'.[53] Payne directly accuses

[53] For more details see Ashis Nandy, 'Final Encounter: The Politics of the Assassination of Gandhi', in *At the Edge of Psychology: Essays on Politics and Culture* (New Delhi: Oxford University Press, 1980), pp. 70–98; and 'Coming

the Bombay police of being involved in the conspiracy to kill Gandhi. Embarrassment and perhaps a touch of guilt pushed them to act more decisively after the assassination. The conspiracy was unearthed soon enough and Savarkar was arrested within eight hours of the assassination. He was tried, along with seven others, for murder. In February 1948, before the trial began, he predictably offered to give another undertaking abjuring politics if let off. The offer was rejected and the trial finally ended the political and intellectual career of this gifted but troubled vendor of hate and violence. However, he 'escaped conviction by the skin of his teeth,' for this time too he had taken his usual care to hide his links with the assassins.[54] Also, some of the most powerful political leaders too wanted Savarkar to be acquitted. Deputy Prime Minister and Minister of Home Affairs Vallabhbhai Patel, for instance, admitted that the government had annoyed the Muslims and 'could not afford to anger the Hindus too.'[55]

Home: Religion, Mass Violence and the Exiled and Secret Selves of a Citizen-Killer', in this volume. Payne in his biography of Gandhi neatly describes the political ambience in which the assassination took place. He talks of the '... shadowy presences lurking in the background. ... Their names are unknown to history, or can be guessed at. The attentive reader of the voluminous trial reports soon finds himself haunted by the certainty that many others who never stood trial were involved in the conspiracy.' Payne, *Life and Death of Mahatma Gandhi*, p. 646.

[54] A.G. Noorani, *Savarkar and Hindutva: The Godse Connection* (New Delhi: LeftWord, 2002), p. 4.

[55] Tushar A. Gandhi, *Let's Kill Gandhi: A Chronicle of His Last Days, the Conspiracy, Murder, Investigation and Trial* (New Delhi: Rupa, 2007), pp. 732–3. Tushar Gandhi also suggests that Patel made peace with his conscience by choosing to believe that Gandhi was killed for going on fast to force the Government of India to give Pakistan the Rs 550 million due to it. Actually, the same group of conspirators had made at least two earlier attempts to kill Gandhi years before the issue of money came up.

Godse—the naïve, ideologically driven killer of Gandhi, pushed by forces that he neither controlled nor fully understood—faced the other Savarkar, the one whom he had not met during his long acquaintance with the guru, only during his trial in 1948. Though he had directly inspired Godse to kill Gandhi, Savarkar now became not merely aloof and distant, he was careful to avoid any show of concern or fraternal feelings towards his protégé, lest it weakened his plea of innocence. Advocate P.L. Inamdar, an admirer of Savarkar who unsuccessfully defended Nathuram's brother Gopal in the same trial, found Savarkar very nervous and agitated during the trial. Savarkar, himself a barrister, repeatedly sought reassurance from Inamdar and asked the lawyer if he would be acquitted; he did not ask a single question about the fate of the others.[56] He was still phobic about jails.

Godse, we learn from those close to him, was deeply hurt. He worshipped Savarkar as a selfless, heroic father figure and was not prepared to discover in the former freedom fighter a self-centred, manipulative politician desperately trying to save his skin. Inamdar says:

> During the various talks I had with Nathuram, he told me that he was deeply hurt by Tatyarao's [Savarkar's] calculated, demonstrative non-association with him either in court or in the Red Fort Jail.... How Nathuram yearned for a touch of Tatyarao's hand, a word of sympathy, or at least a look of compassion ... Nathuram referred to his hurt feelings in this regard even during my last visit with him.[57]

[56] P.L. Inamdar, *The Story of the Red Fort Trial 1948–49* (Bombay: Popular Prakashan, 1979), p. 23.

[57] Ibid., p.14. These details do not support Tushar Gandhi's belief that Savarkar wrote or edited Nathuram Godse's powerfully testimony in court. Gandhi, *Let's Kill Gandhi*, pp. 606–7. However, the testimony does show how deeply the assassin had internalized Savarkar and wanted to act as an extension of Savarkar's self.

Savarkar had reasons to be careful. Though the trial court acquitted him, a judicial enquiry later established his complicity. The Supreme Court judge J.L. Kapur, who headed the enquiry, was clear in his finding: Savarkar *did* lead the conspiracy that killed Gandhi.[58]

The assassination was the last political act of Savarkar. Though he lived another eighteen years, he withdrew into a cell and took care not to offend the government even indirectly. He had already mastered the art of buying peace with authorities. Once in 1950, when he tested waters in the wake of the Nehru-Liaqat Ali Pact and the government frowned upon his political activities, he once again offered to abjure politics to avoid prosecution. When the authorities asked for a formal undertaking, he promptly gave it.[59]

Savarkar died in 1966, a bitter, defeated man. He had fought for the Hindus for nearly sixty years, but the Hindus had failed to appreciate it and had not given him or his party a respectable voice in any election in independent India.[60] The man he had

[58] Justice J.L. Kapur, *Report of Commission of Enquiry into Conspiracy to Murder Mahatma Gandhi* (New Delhi: Government of India Press, 1970), Vol. 2, p. 303.

[59] By this time, giving fawning undertakings to authorities had become a way of life with Savarkar. The last undertaking was also his most abject. In independent India, despite his total opposition to the pact, he promised, in writing, to 'exhort the people to observe the Nehru-Liaqat Ali Pact.' Even his fawning biographer Keer is forced to admit that 'for a moment, the physical agonies [of preventive detention] must have overpowered his stubborn will.' Keer, *Veer Savarkar*, p. 432. This undertaking, too, was given under Morarji Desai, then the Home Minister of Bombay. Understandably Desai, who was in excellent spirits when jailed during the freedom struggle and was to improve in his health when jailed by the Indira Gandhi regime at about the age of 80 during the Emergency and suspension of civil rights in 1975–7, had utter contempt for Savarkar.

[60] Payne puts it succinctly when he says, 'Long before he died, he knew that he had been like a man waiting in the wings for the call to occupy the centre of the stage, but the call never came.' Payne, *Life and Death of Mahatma Gandhi*, p. 209.

loathed for more than fifty years, Gandhi, was triumphant even in death. Not only was he already being called a saint but, horror of horrors, the father of the nation by the same Hindus whom Savarkar had tried so hard to organize as a nation and wean away from the bewitching guiles of the retrogressive counter-modernist and crypto-anarchist. Savarkar, a nineteenth-century European rationalist caught in the hinges of time, could only 'retaliate' by showing his contempt towards his ungrateful compatriots and their fake hero one last time. He declared that he did not want any Hindu rituals after his death and insisted that he should be carried to an electric crematorium, not on human shoulders, as conventions demanded, but on mechanical transport.[61]

ᘒ

It is a peculiar sensation, this double consciousness ... this sense of always looking at one's self through the eyes of another, measuring one's soul by the type of a world that looks on in amused contempt and pity ... two souls, two thoughts, two unreconciled strivings, two warring ideals in one dark body, whose dogged strength alone keeps it from being torn asunder.

W.E.B. Dubois, quoted in Charles Long[62]

Savarkar's life became controversial only after Independence, more so after his death. As details of his role in Gandhi's murder and his obsequious letters to British authorities, seeking forgiveness and promising loyalty, began to get better known, they led to all-round embarrassment. However, that does not fully explain the attempts to undervalue his anti-imperialist record in recent years, why even the fifty-year sentence passed on him is not considered

[61] Keer, *Veer Savarkar*, p. 544.
[62] Charles Long, *Significations: Signs, Symbols, and Images in the Interpretation of Religion* (Aurora, Colorado: The Davies Group, 1995), p. 178.

a proof of his credentials as a freedom fighter. Nor does it explain why there has been so little acceptance that, after being sentenced to jail for fifty years in one's mid-twenties, one may have failure of nerve and collapse of self-esteem. True, the criticisms often come from those who have no direct or indirect link with the freedom struggle against the world's then-reigning superpower and have the luxury of demanding total constancy and persistent self-sacrifice. But it is also true that there has been no enquiry in depth into the inner drives that pushed Savarkar to his particularly petty version of xenophobia. Was his violence an unrealistic, adolescent search for a heroic stature, which collapsed the moment he confronted its 'natural', inevitable consequences under a colonial dispensation? Did the Muslims become for him a safer target, once he sensed the might of the British Empire? Did he represent or tap a political-psychological potentiality in urban, middle-class, Western-educated India? Is that potentiality a price India has paid for its modernization? Are the attempts to demonize Savarkar ultimately a form of exorcism?

The last two questions are especially important. The hostility Savarkar arouses is the hostility towards one who dares to remind us that the post-seventeenth-century idea of nation-state and secularism have both been complicit with ethnoreligious violence during the last two centuries. For Savarkar's hatred for Muslims came not from ideas of ritual purity and impurity or caste hierarchy but from his prognosis of communities that could or could not be integrated—assimilated or dissolved—within the framework of a modern Indian state. The standard conventions of a nation-state within the Westphalian model constituted his religion and he brought to it the fervour of a fundamentalist. He was not willing to wait for the decline of communities, the spread of literacy and urban-industrial values—individuation, secularization, and instrumental rationality—to ensure nation-formation in a society

organized around a different set of principles. He was searching
for something more substantial than territoriality to give Indian
nationalism a stable base. The search was not unknown to modern Indians; many had mounted it before Savarkar and many others were to do so after him. But most of them avoided facing the
full implications of it. Savarkar was more open and honest about
his goals. Hence the periodic obsessive concern in India with the
life of a person who throughout life remained at the margin of
Indian politics and whom mainstream India and Hinduism never
knew well enough to forget.

The second part of the story is the record of secularism
in genocide, particularly ethnonationalist genocide, in recent
times. Data on mass violence show that secular states, backed by
secular ideologies, account for at least two-third of all the deaths
in organized mass violence during the twentieth century.[63] Savarkar
typifies the attitudes and the motivational structure—the genocidal
mentality—that underlies politically engineered mass violence.[64]
The conservative folk theory of secularism in many parts of the
globe, particularly its South Asian variants, cannot cope with
this reality. G.P. Deshpande almost admits defeat when he calls
Savarkar a 'secular communalist' vending a 'supra-religious ideology'; he does not sense how absurd these expressions sound
in South Asian intellectual circles where secularism is seen as
a magical cure of all communal passions.[65] Nor is Deshpande
willing to take the next step and read Savarkar as a pathological

---

[63] See, for example, R.J. Rummel, *Death by Government: Genocide and Mass
Murder Since 1900* (West Hanover, Mass.: Christopher Publishing, 1994).
[64] See, for example, Robert Jay Lifton and Eric Markusen, *The Genocidal Mentality: Nazi Holocaust and the Nuclear Threat* (New York: Basic, 1990).
[65] G.P. Deshpande, 'An Occasion for the RSS', *Economic and Political Weekly*,
25 March 2006. Deshpande also points out that Savarkar conceptualized
Hindutva as some kind of Hegelian Geist. It is not clear from his brief but

by-product of the modern idea of a secular nation-state rather than that of Hinduism.

The love–hate relationship with Savarkar in sections of India's urban middle-class and the political identity he offered can be read, more aptly, as a lesson on the limits of nineteenth-century modernity, scientific rationality, and political realism rather than as pathological ethnophobia. He was one person who had grasped the scope modern rationality offered to act out the hate within him and his attitudes to Hindutva and the Hindus were as instrumental as his attitude towards the Muslims. His rationalist, amoral, anti-religious self had paradoxically arrived at the conclusion that only religion could be an efficacious building block for nation- and state-formation in South Asia and he did not know where to stop. In his impersonal, reified, Brahminic ideas of state-craft and politics, there was not much place for emotions, certainly not for compassion. The aloof ruthlessness came packaged in an arrogant trust in his own cleverness and strategizing skills.[66]

Even Savarkar's atheism was not the philosophical atheism associated with Buddhism, Lokayata, and Vedanta, but the anti-clerical, hard atheism of fin-de-siècle scientism, increasingly popular among sections of the European middle-class and, through cultural osmosis, in parts of modern India.[67] His politics paralleled the way European racism in the 1940s drew upon modern science,

---

insightful comment whether Savarkar borrowed as directly from Hegel as he did from Mazzini.

[66] For a brief but not a satisfactory discussion of this issue, see Ashis Nandy, 'Adorns in India: Revisiting the Psychology of Fascism', in *At the Edge of Psychology* (New Delhi: Oxford University Press, 1980), pp. 99–111.

[67] Nothing expressed Savarkar's tough-minded atheism better than his refusal to allow any Hindu religious ritual or rite when his wife died, notwithstanding public protests and *satyagraha* by some of his followers. He did not want even her body to be brought home, saying that it was 'no use lamenting over the dead body.' Keer, *Veer Savarkar*, pp. 529–30.

particularly nineteenth-century biology and eugenics, and saw itself responsible for doing the dirty work of scientized history.[68] The sceptics might like to look up Savarkar's comments on the cow, worshipped as sacred by most Hindus, and compare it with the position of the organizations and parties that constitute the Hindu nationalist formation today. While the latter try to pander to the sentiments of the Hindus, Savarkar publicly supported cow slaughter when necessary and declared the cow to be a useless animal with no sacredness about it.[69] He also advised Hindus to give up vegetarianism and eat fish and eggs.[70] When Gandhi's assassin and Savarkar's protégé Godse complained in his last testament in court about Gandhi's 'superstitious' use of ideas like soul force and fasting in modern politics, it was not the accusation of a Hindu fundamentalist. It mirrored Savarkar's statism.

[68] Aditya Nigam in a comment has differentiated between two styles of Hindu nationalism, one typified by Savarkar and the other by Golwalkar, arguably the first believing Hindu who came to head the RSS in the 1940s. He suggests that Golwalkar's is the more dangerous version. Aditya Nigam, 'Reading between the Chinks in Pariwar Armour', Tehelka, 25 June 2005, p. 20. Nigam may be right, because the likes of Golwalkar can take Hindu nationalism into Hinduism and reshape the culture of Indian politics and, at the end, Hinduism in a way that Savarkar could never do. On the other hand, Savarkar seems to conform more faithfully to the profile of the fascist personality as portrayed in post-World War II psychoanalysis and social and political psychology. Could it be that, despite the rhetoric of public debate in India, the 'classical' European fascism in India can be the ideology of only a conspiratorial political fringe and the more dangerous sources of political authoritarianism lie elsewhere?

[69] Dayananda Saraswati, the founder of Arya Samaj, also approved of eating beef in the first edition of Satyārthaprakāsh (1874) but the remark was dropped from the second edition in 1882. P.C. Ghosh, The Development of Indian National Congress (1892–1909) (Calcutta: Firma K.L. Mukhopadhyay, 1960), quoted in Sharma, 'Savarkar's Quest for a Modern Hindu Consolidation', p.69. As is well-known, similar comments are attributed to Vivekananda, too.

[70] Keer, Veer Savarkar, pp. 443–4.

Over the last eighty years, most ideologues of Hindu nationalism have neither come from orthodox Hinduism nor have they flaunted their orthodoxy the way Gandhi did, by proclaiming himself a Sanatani Hindu. They have proudly affirmed their links with the nineteenth-century Hindu reform movements, which they see as analogues of a masculine Protestantism, cleaning up a degraded, distorted faith to make it fit the needs of a national state.

These ideologues borrowed from ideas that were in the air during their formative years. Not only among European fascists but also among the European intelligentsia in general and among Westernized Indians trying desperately to cope with their feelings of inferiority and attain global respectability through tough-minded, secular rationality wedded to ideas of national interest, social evolutionism, political realism, and progressivism. Savarkar's contempt for the likes of Gandhi came partly from that. Savarkar was not alone. The first head of the RSS, Keshav Baliram Hedgewar (1889–1940), too, could hardly be called a run-of-the-mill, believing Hindu. An urban, well-educated, modern doctor, with poor links with rural India and mainstream Hinduism, he, like many pioneers of Hindu nationalism, was an aggressive critic of Hinduism and was exposed to religious and social reform movements, especially the Ramakrishna Mission founded in 1897 by Swami Vivekananda (1863–1902). Hindu nationalism, on this plane, was popular European political theory and political history telescoped into South Asia as a form of toady Hinduism. In retrospect one realizes why Gandhi insisted that the nineteenth-century religious reform movements had done more harm than good to Hinduism in the long run.

The entire process has remarkable parallels with the experiences of Sri Lankan Buddhism and Indian Islam under colonialism and the dual impact of urbanization and industrialization. There is in them the same efforts to rationalize one's faith and to set up demonic others who seemed better equipped to handle the demands of modern world and its amoral ways; they too, consequently, initiated the same kind of self-engineering to be able to flirt with the Dionysian in human personality. [71] As if they were all caught in a larger, inescapable, evolutionary process that enjoyed intrinsic legitimacy even among those hostile to religious nationalism.[72] That partly explains why most conservative Muslim clerics in India opposed the idea of a separate country for South Asian Muslims as un-Islamic, whereas the leadership of the Pakistan movement sought a modern Muslim state, the way many secular, liberal Jews sought a Jewish state. Is the dream of a liberal, ethnonationalist, modern state sustainable in the long run? Or is it an oxymoron? No final answer has yet been given.

The founder of Pakistan, Mohammad Ali Jinnah—Westernized, loyal to constitutionalism, staunchly secular in personal life—had as his avowed role model the classical liberal Gopal Krishna Gokhale (1866–1915). Jinnah kept the *ulema* at a distance throughout life, but was perfectly willing to use them to advance the cause of a separate homeland for South Asian Muslims. Exactly as Savarkar, despite all his anti-Muslim rhetoric

[71] See, for instance, Stanley J. Tambiah, *Buddhism Betrayed? Religion, Politics and Violence in Sri Lanka* (Chicago: University of Chicago, 1992); and T.N. Madan, *Modern Myths, Locked Minds: Secularism and Fundamentalism in India* (New Delhi: Oxford University Press, 1998). The overall cultural psychological framework within which Savarkar worked has been discussed in Ashis Nandy, Shikha Trivedi, Achyut Yagnik, and Shail Mayaram, *Creating a Nationality: The Ramjanmabhumi Movement and Fear of the Self* (New Delhi: Oxford University Press, 1995).

[72] For instance, the early Hindu nationalists were role models for Sri Lankan Buddhist nationalists. Anagarika Dhammapala (1864–1933) lived in Calcutta, the capital of British India till 1911 and was an admirer of Vivekananda. The Mahabodhi Society that Dhammapala established was directly inspired by the Ramakrishna Mission and less directly by the Theosophical Society.

and passion for united India, established coalitions in Sindh and Bengal with the Muslim League, fighting for Pakistan, and proudly declared these alliances to be more nationalistic than the ministries formed by the 'pseudo-nationalist' Indian National Congress, led by Gandhi and Nehru.[73] There *are* parallels between the trajectories Savarkar and Jinnah traversed and the reason they chose religion as a vehicle of nation-building despite being non-believers or casual believers. Both had internalized contemporary European political categories and saw nationality as a crucial module of sovereign, modern republics. Both sought to replicate in South Asia existing wisdom in the global citadels of knowledge. Both represented the triumph in the South not so much of history as of European history. If they were fundamentalists, their fundamentals came from conventional European wisdom about nation-building and state-formation. Defying the warning of Rabindranath Tagore, they owned up the 'motive force' of Western nationalism as their own.[74] Not surprisingly, the personal relationship between Savarkar and Jinnah never soured. Nor did Savarkar ever entirely lose the respect of the likes of Subhas Chandra Bose, M.N. Roy, and B.R. Ambedkar.

ॐ

I have used some scrappy biographical details on Savarkar to pose a series of questions: Has it become more or less inevitable for a social group—be it a religion, caste, denomination, sect, or ethnicity—to gradually acquire the features of a nationality because that seems the only way community grievances can be aggregated and effectively articulated in cultures of state

[73] Savarkar and Joshi, *Historical Statements by V.D. Savarkar*, pp. 96–105; esp. pp. 99–101.
[74] Rabindranath Tagore, *Nationalism* (London: Macmillan, 1917), pp. 77–8.

in which the ideas of citizenship and of nationality are deeply enmeshed? Do claims made in the name of a nationality have more political impact than the same claims made in the name of other aggregates and, as a result, has there grown, in the last hundred years, a tendency in religious or ethnic political formations to act as nationalities to empower themselves? Does that allow more effective mobilization in modernizing societies, particularly among the newly modern, uprooted by social changes and seeking new communities, real or imaginary? Does it also mean that such nationalism has natural limits in a society that is not fully modern? Does Savarkar's marginalization in Hindu society have something to tell us?[75]

Everyone knows that the Western history of state-formation and nation-building is simultaneously a story of how religions, denominations, and ethnicities were bludgeoned into nationalities. For those entering the realm of history for the first time in Asia and Africa—and facing the hierarchies and exclusions of the global state-nation system for the first time—the temptation is not only to construct their own history, but also to read into Europe's history their own past, present, and future. Even when they construct their own history, the categories and concerns that frame it are 'universal' or, it comes to the same thing, European. When that reading is deployed as an evolutionary grid in an Asian or African society, there is a vague but acute fear that unless one builds a nation, whatever its cost in human suffering, one will not get justice locally or globally.

[75] I should clarify at this point that I view nationalism as an ideology that is radically different from the sentiment called patriotism, though the first kind of territoriality may build upon or mobilize for its purposes the second kind. For a more extended discussion of the issue, see Nandy, 'Nationalism, Genuine and Spurious: A Very Late Obituary of Two Early Post-Nationalist Strains in India', pp. 1–18 in this volume.

Vinayak Damodar Savarkar and Mohammed Ali Jinnah were not personally as culpable as many like to believe. The evil that many locate in them resided, at least partly, in the political ideas that dominated the world. Savarkar and Jinnah were, like most first-generation builders of South Asian states, faithful and obedient pupils of the Bismarckian state and post-medieval European republicanism, both vital parts of the dominant culture of common sense in their times. Once they accepted that culture, they could not but try to duplicate Europe's history in South Asia, whatever the cost. Not surprisingly, neither of the two is known to have ever mourned the unnecessary death of more than a million people in the bloodbath that came with the division of British India.[76] For both, human beings were means of implementing important historical designs and in their versions of nationalism the sufferings of the nations they represented were probably only instances of collateral damage. The rationality they worshipped overlay deep emotional voids, created by personal losses that came almost like betrayals by fate. Both coped with the betrayal through uncompromising, dispassionate, ruthless pursuit of a form of political rationality that allowed and even glorified withdrawal from or avoidance of personal emotional involvements.[77]

[76] I have already drawn attention to Savarkar's fascination with gratuitous violence in political matters. That fascination, though it came packaged in the rhetoric of revolution, preceded his ideological convictions. Many have found more disorienting the openness to violence of Jinnah, whom Eqbal Ahmad has called a liberal constitutionalist. Eqbal Ahmad, *Confronting Empire*, Interviews with David Barsamian (London: Pluto Press, 2000), p. 10. Kuldip Nayar, for instance, says that when asked in 1946, after the call for Direct Action given by the Muslim League, whether Direct Action would be violent or non-violent, Jinnah said, 'I am not going to discuss ethics.' Kuldip Nayar, *Scoop: Inside Stories from the Partition to the Present* (New Delhi: HarperCollins, 2006), p. 25.

[77] See Salman Akhtar and Manasi Kumar, 'Destiny and Nationalism: Mohammad Ali Jinnah', in Salman Akhtar (ed.), *The Crescent and the*

Both lived with fragile, perhaps anchorless self-definitions that pushed them to embrace aggressive, ideological postures that tallied with their deeper psychological needs. As I have said, in politics if you wear a mask long enough, it becomes your face.

Jinnah's case was more tragic. In his famous speech of 11 August 1947, three days before the birth of Pakistan, he declared inclusive nationalism based on territoriality as his project and sought to distinguish between inclusive and sectoral nationalism exactly the way Jawaharlal Nehru did.[78] He wanted Pakistan not to exclude non-Muslims in principle and in practice. Himself a Shia, Jinnah included in Pakistan's first cabinet an Ahmadiya as the foreign minister and a Hindu Dalit as the minister of law.[79] Pakistan's first national anthem was written by a Hindu and, it is said, Jinnah had a hand in that choice. These did not help; it was too late or, perhaps, too early. Nor could Indian nationalism, despite the presence of leaders such as Jawaharlal Nehru, avoid full-scale militarization, nuclearism, and intermittent religious and ethnonationalist violence. Nationalism, once let out of the bag, tends to become self-sustaining and plots its own political-psychological agenda.

Many Southern scholars, blinded by nationalism's anti-imperialist role in the South, believe it can be tamed and used creatively. The experiences of South Asia in the last two centuries

---

Couch: Cross-Currents Between Islam and Psychoanalysis (Lanham, Maryland: Jason Aronson, 2008), pp. 79–102.

[78] Jinnah's first Presidential Address to the Constituent Assembly of Pakistan, 11 August 1947, http://www.pakistani.org/pakistan/legislation_address_11aug1947.html (accessed on 31 August 2015).

[79] It is remarkable that the passage of modern, secular constitutions of both India and Pakistan were officially piloted by two Dalits, Babasaheb Ambedkar and Jogen Mandal. The former, who of course played a more significant role in shaping the constitution of his country, is virtually deified in India; the latter is forgotten in both countries.

suggest that sometimes, in some sections of society, religions and cultures change to accommodate nationalism, not the other way round. Savarkar, whom many see as a minor pawn of South Asian history, did change not only South Asian Hinduism but also South Asian Islam and Buddhism. All three had to accommodate strains that had more in common with house-broken versions of Christianity in Europe and North America than with home-grown South Asian Hinduism, Islam, and Buddhism.[80]

Ultimately, Vinayak Damodar Savarkar is the name of a blown-up, grotesque temptation inherent in the Southern world's encounter with the global nation-state system and with religious traditions that facilitate the internalization of the core principles of Western nationalism. That temptation is a part of everyone dreaming of working with tamed versions of nationalism armed with ideas of rationality, secularism, progress, and the so-called lessons of history, fearful of being trapped by empathy, compassion, and other such unworthy concerns.

[80] For instance, E. Valentine Daniel, 'The Arrogation of Being by the Blind-Spot of Religion', *Hitotsubashi Journal of Social Studies*, July 2001, 33(1), pp. 83–102. True, surveys done in India suggest that only about 10 per cent of those who vote for Hindu nationalist parties do so on ideological grounds, but in absolute numbers that is a substantial presence. Data Unit of the Centre for the Study of Developing Societies, 1998 Survey of General Elections in India.

Coming Home

Religion, Mass Violence, and the Exiled and Secret Selves of a Citizen-killer

The violence that broke out when British India was partitioned into India and Pakistan killed at least a million. Yet, there were no criminal enquiries, arrests, court cases, or convictions associated with the killings, rapes, mutilations, arson, and pillage. Partition took place when human rights movements were more or less unknown, in a world just getting accustomed to genocide and ethnic cleansing and the wanton destructiveness of the two World Wars. Ideologically driven, handy justifications of such violence were still floating around in the global culture of knowledge. The main ideological movements in the world were all perfectly comfortable with the idea of bloodshed as a part of normal politics. The civilizing mission of colonialism, the pursuit of national interest, revolutionary violence and people's war, even the concepts of reason and scientific rationality that were brought to bear upon public affairs through social evolutionism, eugenics, and 'scientized' history—they all enjoyed wide legitimacy not merely among political actors but also among the intelligentsia. Even those who fought against the psychopathic violence of European authoritarianism in the name of democracy contributed handsomely to the culture of violence.

Understandably, neither the British-Indian government nor the successor states of India and Pakistan ever tried to apprehend the killers or launch criminal investigations into the violence of Partition. In any case, efforts to do so would have been futile. The police and law enforcement agencies were hopelessly compromised; their partisan behaviour and, sometimes, direct collusion with the mobs are well-known to anyone who has talked with any victim of the violence. And the violence was decentralized enough for the state to be primarily a spectator. The only central force that seemed to function during the period was the personality, and the political and moral presence of Mohandas Karamchand Gandhi, whom the last British Viceroy, Louis Mountbatten, called a one-man boundary force. It is in this sense that Mahmood Mamdani's tentative formulation that the violence of 1946–8, like the genocide in Rwanda in 1994, could be called a popular genocide has its appeal.

We may agree that genocidal violence cannot be understood as rational, yet, we need to understand it as thinkable. Rather than run away from it, we need to realize that it is the 'popularity' of the genocide that is its uniquely troubling aspect. In its social aspect, Hutu/Tutsi violence in the Rwandan genocide invites comparison with Hindu/ Muslim violence at the time of the partition of colonial India. Neither can be explained as simply a state project. One shudders to put the words 'popular' and 'genocide' together, therefore I put 'popularity' in quotation marks. And yet, one needs to explain the large-scale civilian involvement in the genocide. To do so is to contextualize it, to understand the logic of its development.[1]

It is now well-known—after Hannah Arendt, Robert J. Lifton, and Zygmunt Bauman—that data do not support the early efforts to interpret the European genocide as the work of sadists, criminals, and psychopaths. True, a small proportion of the killers can be classified as psychological and social misfits, but the work of annihilation involved a much larger social segment that squarely falls within the range of normality as conventionally defined.

> By conventional criteria no more than 10 per cent of the SS could be considered 'abnormal'. This observation fits the general trend of testimony by survivors. ... Our judgement is that the overwhelming majority of SS men, leaders as well as rank and file, would have easily passed all the psychiatric tests ordinarily given to American army recruits or Kansas City policemen.[2]

If the killers are not outside the range of normality, how are genocides organized? After all, killing does not come naturally to human beings. The skill has to be painstakingly inculcated. Following political psychologist Herbert Kelman, Zygmunt Bauman suggests three conditions that weaken moral restraints on violence and cruelty: when violence is authorized and official, when violent behaviour is routinized and demanded as part

[1] Mahmood Mamdani, *When Victims Become Killers: Colonialism, Nativism and the Genocide in Rwanda* (Kampala: Fountain Publishers, 2001), p. 8.
[2] George M. Kren and Leon Rappoport, *The Holocaust and the Crisis of Human Behaviour* (New York: Holmes and Meier, 1980), p. 2; quoted in Zygmunt Bauman, *Modernity and the Holocaust* (Cambridge, UK: Polity Press, 1989), p. 19.

of a role, and when victims of violence are dehumanized through ideological indoctrination of the perpetrators.[3]

We explore here how, when genocide becomes thinkable to ordinary, otherwise law-abiding citizens, it is not the end of the story. They have to cope with this other self which preceded the genocide and the way it handled differences in cultures and faiths.

One of the more influential works in recent years on the second part of the story—routinization of violence and socialization into violence as a way of life—is Dave Grossman's *On Killing*.[4] Grossman is not a social psychologist like Milgram but a soldier-scholar who comes from the heart of the American military machine and has taught at the US Military Academy. He not only tells how violence get routinized into normality, but also, contra-Milgram, how difficult it is to weaken the inner resistance to killing in human beings and how much effort has to go into that weakening.

Dehumanization of victim community can be read as part of the larger process that Lifton calls psychological numbing, though numbing is obviously not unrelated to the other two contributing factors. Such dehumanization is usually brought about through hate propaganda, manipulation of history to set up the victims as intrinsically dangerous or contaminating, and the use of scientific or pseudo-scientific categories such as eugenics, demography, and social evolutionism.

[3] Bauman, *Modernity and the Holocaust*. For the first two conditions, Kelman is of course heavily indebted to Stanley Milgram, *Obedience to Authority: An Experimental View* (New York: Harper and Row, 1974). See also Herbert C. Kelman and V. Lee Hamilton, Crimes of Obedience: *Toward a Social Psychology of Authority and Responsibility* (New York: Yale University Press, 1990).

[4] Dave Grossman, *On Killing: The Psychological Cost of Learning to Kill in War and Society* (Boston: Little, Brown, 1995); see particularly Ch. 1–2.

However, even after all such manoeuvres, it is not easy for the perpetrators and passively complicit citizenry to erase their moral discomfort after an instance of mass violence or genocide. The inner resistance to killing and torture is a part of human self-definition and, except for confirmed psychopaths, all participants in mass violence have to learn to live with themselves. Indeed, it is doubtful whether even psychopaths are as successful in liberating themselves from moral restraints as psychiatrists and clinical psychologists believe. G.M. Gilbert, the prison psychologist at the Nuremberg trial of Nazi criminals, calls Herman Goering 'a moral coward' and a psychopath and goes on to tell what he said to Goering about Goering's responses to the Rorschach inkblot test: 'Do you remember the card with the red spot? Well, morbid neurotics often hesitate over that card and then say there's blood on it. You hesitated, but you did not call it blood. *You tried to flick off with your finger*, as though you thought you could wipe away the blood with a little gesture.'[5]

But Goering *did* try to flick off the blood and it *did* seem to Gilbert that what he said to Goering had struck home.[6] If that happens with one of the most notorious killers of the twentieth century, it should be safe to presume that a normal person who takes part in mass violence has to cope with the killer within him.[7] That is what I explore here. For when genocide becomes thinkable to ordinary, otherwise law-abiding citizens, they have to live with the persistence of that other self they leave behind, not only

[5] G.M. Gilbert, *Nuremberg Diary* (New York: Farrar, Straus, 1947), p. 435.
[6] Ibid.
[7] See also Gilbert's notes on the reactions of the Nazi leaders to the documentary films on German concentration camps, shown during their trial. Acute moral distress in some of them was obvious and at least two of them cried. Ibid., pp. 45–7.

during their journey through violence, but even when they walk
out of it.

ɛʌ

This is the story of an unapologetic killer about his past, who also
was a victim of the ethnic cleansing in Punjab during 1946–8,
seething with anger at what had befallen him and the Hindus in
west Punjab. Like many others, he held Mohandas Karamchand
Gandhi personally responsible for their suffering and for appeas-
ing the Muslims. Overtly impenitent, he nonetheless had to erect
a barricade of defences that separated his earlier self from what
he claimed he had since become. But the defences were not fool-
proof. Despite full support from his political ideology, he had not
been able to buy peace. As in the case of some other killers who
deployed a roughly similar technology of distancing, behind the
façade of what he claimed he had to do as part of personal duty
and nationalist responsibility, there were desperate attempts to
sustain a complicated form of doubling.[8] What at first looked like
inner contradictions and hypocrisy, began to look at the end like
a painful, incomplete return journey.

The Remembered Past

Madanlal Pahwa was arguably the most notorious refugee
to come to India from Pakistan in the wake of the violence
of Partition. For he was one of the conspirators who assassinated

[8] See, on the subject of doubling, Robert J. Lifton, *Nazi Doctors: Medical Killing
and the Psychology of Genocide* (New York: Basic Books, 1986); and 'Reflections on Genocide', *Psychohistorical Review*, 1986, 14, pp. 39–54.

Mohandas Karamchand Gandhi on 30 January 1948. Pahwa threw a bomb at a prayer meeting of Gandhi five days before the assassination, which was to be followed by an attack on Gandhi. But the would-be assassin got cold feet and Gandhi lived for another five days. Nathuram Godse, the person who finally pulled the trigger, said during his trial that they had to kill Gandhi for betraying the interests of the Hindus and the state of India by being partial towards the Muslims and pushing his hare-brained ideas of soul force, non-violence, fasting, and counter-modernity.[9]

Pahwa was caught almost immediately after he threw the bomb and it would have been easy for the police to crack the assassination plot and track down the plotters. But they did not move fast enough. They worked in an atmosphere of widespread hostility to Gandhi in an India plagued by religious violence and growing discomfort in the urban, modernizing middle-class with Gandhi and his 'strange' ideas of cross-national amity and non-violent politics, which looked like burdens on 'normal' statecraft. The Delhi police itself had been blatantly partial during the riots at Delhi.[10] The anti-Gandhi sentiments were strongest among the Hindu refugees from west Punjab.[11]

The police, however, moved quickly after the assassination to unearth the plot and the conspirators. They filed a suit against

---

[9] See more details in Ashis Nandy, 'Final Encounter: The Politics of the Assassination of Gandhi', in *At the Edge of Psychology: Essays in Politics and Culture* (New Delhi: Oxford University Press, 1980), pp. 70–98.

[10] One indicator of this hostility to Gandhi was the support mobilized by the Defence Committee set up to fight the case for the assassins. According to Pahwa, it raised between Rs 3,00,000 and 4,00,000—a tidy sum in those days. For a brief discussion of the political culture within which the assassination become possible, see Nandy, 'Final Encounter.'

[11] Manohar Malgonkar, *The Men Who Killed Gandhi* (Delhi: Orient Paperbacks, 1981), Ch.1.

the seven persons involved, including Pahwa, who at the end of
the trial was sentenced to life imprisonment. Life imprisonment
in India did not then mean a jail sentence of fourteen years, as
it does now. The convicts were released after seventeen years in
1965. Pahwa was twenty-one when he went to jail and thirty-
eight when he came out of it. During these years, none of his rela-
tives came to see him, not even his father who lived close to the
various jails where his son was.

When I met Pahwa in 1998–9, he was a forgotten man. It
was with some difficulty that I found his address and phone
number. When I began searching for him, a few actually said that
he was probably dead, even though he had been rediscovered
once in a while by enterprising journalists in the previous three
decades. Pahwa was no longer relevant to Indian politics, not
even to its Hindu nationalist version.

It was difficult to get an appointment with Pahwa. He was
unwell and his kidneys were failing him. He had to undergo dialysis twice a week. However, his lust for life was intact. Though in
his mid-seventies, whenever I called him, he sounded confident
that he would recover fully within a few weeks. He asked me to
be patient. Dialysis made him feel weak and he might not be his
usual self, he said. I had to persuade him to meet me because,
having talked with his wife on phone about his health, I was less
optimistic about his recovery.

My two brief encounters with Pahwa took place in 1998–9,
both times at his office. He ran a small, nondescript firm called
Commercial Services, from a tiny room behind the shops at
Ranade Road, Dadar, Bombay (now Mumbai). It was primarily
an employment agency. He looked like any other nondescript,
elderly man who blended with the modest surroundings of
his office. He wore crumpled clothes, in which he had probably
slept before my arrival, and looked clearly unwell.

Both the interviews had to be terminated after about thirty minutes, though I stayed back to either have a chat with his wife or to exchange an occasional word with him while he rested. Both times he felt exhausted and, indeed, looked ill. His wife sat through one of the interviews, while I talked with him mostly about his childhood and his parents. That day his post-dialysis blues were compounded by an upset stomach. (Earlier, I had made another trip to Bombay after fixing an appointment with him from Delhi, but the interview did not take place because he was bed-ridden with high temperature. Another time, a trip to Bombay was cancelled at the last moment because he was again unwell.)

It gradually dawned on me that Pahwa's prognosis of his own health was not reliable and I had to find someone in Bombay to interview him at short notice. It was then that I approached Rajni Bakshi, distinguished journalist, activist-scholar, and the author of *Bapu Kuti*, a well-known book on Gandhi's successors in India, to interview Pahwa.[12] A conversation between a Gandhian scholar-activist and one of Gandhi's killers might be rewarding, I thought. Also, Bakshi belonged to a Punjabi family, which, though settled at Bombay, was never far from Partition violence. The following section is based mainly on the interviews done by Bakshi and my occasional interpretations of the exchanges that took place between the two.

৩

When Bakshi met Madanlal Pahwa, she found him lying prone in his office. His wife and a few others were present. They had a tape

---

[12] Rajni Bakshi, *Bapu Kuti: Journeys in Rediscovery of Gandhi* (New Delhi: Penguin, 1998).

recorder and the entire session was recorded.[13] It was Tuesday.
The previous day, Pahwa had undergone his routine dialysis.
Bakshi was greeted with much warmth and after a brief introduction—she was there, she said, to continue the conversation
initiated by me—they talked for about 75 minutes. Later Bakshi
interviewed him again.

Madanlal Pahwa was born in 1927 and grew up in Pakpattan, a
small town in Montgomery district in Punjab. The town is now in
Pakistan. His father, Kashmirilal, was a government servant, working in what Madanlal called the 'Colony Department', presumably
the department that looked after the canal colonies in Punjab during colonial times. Kashmirilal was twenty-one years old when his
first wife died. Madanlal was their only child. He remarried and
had several other children with whom Madanlal was still in touch.
Young Madan's relationship with his stepmother was not good and
his relationship with his father, who did not believe in sparing the
rod and spoiling the child, was not much better.

Madanlal claimed to be an active member of the Hindu
nationalist organization, the Rashtriya Swayamsevak Sangh or
RSS, since the age of six. This may not be as precocious as it
sounds, since the RSS *shakhās* or branches served both as centres for ideological indoctrination and gyms for the urban, lower-
middle-class youth lacking facilities for physical exercise. When
asked what had attracted him to the RSS at such a young age,
Madanlal said, 'discipline, physical exercise and games. I thor-
oughly enjoyed going to the shākhā even though my father used
to beat me for going there, because it was anti-government.'

Madanlal remembered his school days warmly. They were
the best phase of his life, he said. But his description of his

[13] My interviews were recorded only by me. Probably because Bakshi was a
well-known journalist and the family perhaps expected her to write a column
based on the interviews.

school days did not fully bear this out. In his school there were organized gangs of Hindu and Muslim boys. Of course, there was friendship between Hindu and Muslim students, but the gangs were also there. Madanlal led one gang and the nephew of the head of the local *mazār* (tomb) led another. Once, when Madan was in the eighth or ninth class, the other gang attacked a boy in Madan's gang with a knife. Madanlal's gang then 'beat up four of them'. Then, he in turn got beaten at home for his violence. Later, the head of the richest Hindu family in town, and the senior-most minister, Diwan, at *the* mazār met and resolved the quarrel. As we shall see, there were other things in Pakpattan that he remembered with greater nostalgia and warmth, but he also wanted to remember his adolescent delinquencies as early signs of his ideological fervour.

Young Madan loved food—'I used to eat so much that people used to call me a *rākshasa* [ogre].' Food also was plentiful and cheap in Montgomery. They included fruits, green vegetables, nuts, and sweetmeats. Pahwa attributed his capacity to withstand the illness of his old age to Pakpattan food. The imagery of a utopian, bucolic existence in pre-Partition days—organized around memories of nature's bounty, particularly the abundance of food, its purity and quality—was a running theme among the uprooted we interviewed and other studies of Partition, too, have found a similar pattern.[14] These memories, one suspects, were a means of

[14] See Dipesh Chakrabarty, 'Remembered Villages: Representation of Hindu-Bengali Memories in the Aftermath of the Partition', *Economic and Political Weekly*, 10 August 1996, pp. 2143–51; Gyanendra Pandey, 'Partition and Independence at Delhi: 1947–48', *Economic and Political Weekly*, 6 September 1997, 32(36), pp. 2261–72; and Ashis Nandy, 'The Invisible Holocaust and the Journey as an Exodus: The Poisoned Village and the Stranger City', in *An Ambiguous Journey to the City: The Village and Other Odd Ruins of the Self in the Indian Imagination* (New Delhi: Oxford University Press, 2001), p. 133.

coping with the memories of the traumatic events that were to follow. For Pahwa, the memories acquired a sharper edge because the creation of Pakistan—literally, a place of purity or a place for the pure and, thus, a synonym of Pakpattan—meant not merely the loss of a paradise but also the alienation of the most valued part of his self.

When Bakshi asked about other aspects of his life in Pakpattan, Pahwa claimed, rather incongruously, that they were *kattar* or hardcore Hindus. This could be defensive, cultural self-assertion or a retrospective attempt to establish some continuity between his childhood and later politics, for he then drifted into memories that conveyed an altogether different impression. The mazār of Baba Fareed Shakarganj at Pakpattan dominated his memories of Pakpattan. The mazār attracted people from faraway places and every year there was a four-day fair around it. On one of the four days there was a procession and it was the only day that the *bahisht darwāzā* (heaven's gate) of the mazār was opened to the public. The best *qawwāls* came to sing at the mazār and the singing went on till late into the night. Deena Qawwāl was one of the finest among those who sang.

Young Madan used to sneak out of home late at night to join his friends and listen to these *qawwālis*. The listeners, he said, included both Hindus and Muslims. Bakshi found that he had particularly vivid memories of the force and passion of the qawwāli singers and remembered with much feeling and painfully sweet nostalgia the joy of it all. He even remembered a couplet from one of the qawwālis:

Salām usko jisne bādshāhi mein fakiri ki
Salām usko ki jisne gāliyan sunkar duāin di.

I salute the one who when a king lives as an ascetic
I salute the one who answers invectives with blessings.

The memories of the shared shrine, the Sufi music, and the overall ambience of the mazār had left a deep impression on him. They remained the pivot of his memories of Pakpattan.

When Bakshi asked him why then there was a conflict between Hindus and Muslims, Pahwa promptly said that the Muslim League spread the enmity and the bitterness. The Muslims were otherwise a friendly people ('*Musalmān vaise milansar log the*'). They were artisans and always very respectful towards others ('*badi izzat karte the, hameinshān*'). As craftsmen they also depended on the Hindus. A small minority of Muslims were bad, not all. He went on to say, 'If you want to learn the manners of the cultured people, learn it from the Muslims' ('*Tehzeeb seekhni ho to Musalmān se seekho*'). Pahwa mimicked in slightly ornate, feudal style, what he meant by Muslim good manners: 'Please come in and be seated ('*Āiye tashreef rakhiye*')', adding for good measure, 'If you want to learn the ways of the cultivated, you should get tutored by a [presumably Muslim] courtesan' ('*Tehzeeb seekni ho to kisi kothewāli ke pās jāo*').[15]

In 1944, at the age of seventeen, Madanlal Pahwa ran away from home to avoid harassment by his stepmother and joined the British Indian army. The army sent him to Bombay for training, where he learnt what he called the Indian Observer Code and also to work on wireless. Soon he was promoted and became an officer.[16]

---

[15] This idea of the *tawaif* or the woman in the bordello as the repository of good manners and culture may be found in some other parts of India but seems particularly strong in the refugees from Punjab, who have often continued to live with a sense of loss. See Pran Neville, *Lahore: A Sentimental Journey* (New Delhi: Allied, 1992), particularly the section 'The Splendours of Hiramandi or Tibbi', pp. 53–60.

[16] Some biographical accounts give a different version. They say that Madanlal was actually rejected by the army and, though he had a temporary government job that had something to do with the war effort, it had nothing directly to do with the army. See Malgonkar, *The Men Who Killed Gandhi*.

At Bombay, he remained active in the RSS shākhā at Shivaji Park. There he met Jagdish Chandra Jain and one Azad, whose full name he could not remember.

After a while he was posted at Lahore where he got further training in sending and receiving cables. Presumably, it was a short-term commission, for he retired in 1947 at the age of twenty. By the time he was, he said, a second lieutenant. His entitlements as an ex-serviceman helped him to get admission into a college at Lahore. However, he could not join the college. Partition forced him and his family to leave for India.

Like most refugees from west Punjab, Pahwa came to India as part of a *kafila* or caravan from Pakpattan. They crossed the river Sutlej at Bangla-phazil and reached Fazilka and then Ferozpur, where his mother's sister lived. Father Kashmirilal and some other members of his family came to India separately by train. The train was attacked on the way. Kashmirilal was injured but recovered after treatment in a hospital at Ferozpur. Madanlal's youngest bother survived because he got buried under several dead bodies and was left for dead. Only his father's sister was killed in the Partition violence. The rest made it to India safely.

Madanlal did not describe these experiences in detail, perhaps because he had given a moving account of them during his trial under oath: 'We walked night and day. There were men and women of all ages and all conditions. Many could not stand the strain. They—mostly women and children—were left on the road.' As for his father's experience, he said, 'Only 40 or 50 survived out of 400 or 500 and even these were in hospitals. My aunt had been killed, more than a hundred girls abducted, my father rescued from a heap of the dead.'[17] There were occasional

---

[17] Madanlal Pahwa, Testimony at Court during the Gandhi Murder Trial, quoted in Malgonkar, *The Men Who Killed Gandhi*, p. 17.

exaggerations and propaganda, too, in the testimony. Pahwa claimed that he saw in Fazilka a column of refugees 40 miles long and another in which marched 'five hundred women who had been stripped naked' and 'women with their breasts, noses, ears and cheeks cut. ... One of them told me how her child was roasted and she was asked to partake of the same.'[18]

By then, Madanlal said, Kashmirilal's former boss in Pakpattan was on Prime Minister Nehru's staff. Kashmirilal gave Madanlal a letter addressed to the officer, requesting that Madanlal be enrolled in the police. The son had other ideas; he tore up the letter. When the conditions in the country were so bad, he could not work for the government, he said to Bakshi.

In 1947, Madanlal Pahwa moved to Gwalior with his maternal aunt. There he began to work with the Hindu Rashtra Sena, a wing of the Hindu Mahasabha. The main person in the group was one Dr Dattatraya Parchure, who would later join the conspiracy to murder Gandhi. In Gwalior, Pahwa also became friendly with a man called Shivpuri and together they formed a group that attacked Muslims on the streets of the city, 'because they were killing our people coming in trains from Pakistan.' (The 'they' here does not of course refer to the Gwalior Muslims, but the unknown killers of the Hindus escaping from west Punjab. Some of these killers were victims of violence who had escaped from India.) The group that Pahwa joined also attacked a train packed with Muslims going from Gwalior to Bhopal and killed many of the travellers. He said he used a pistol and hand grenades for the purpose, not knives or swords.

Pahwa criticized Gandhi for implicating the Maharaja of Bhopal in these attacks by accusing the state administration of colluding with the killers. The head of the Bhopal state was not

[18] Ibid.

a Hindu Maharaja but a Muslim Nawab. Pahwa probably had
in mind the Maharaja of Gwalior. That would tally with the fact
that the head of Gwalior police told Pahwa and his associates
to run away or else the police would have to arrest them. That
also suggests that perhaps Gandhi was not wrong in his accusation. Anyhow, Pahwa moved to Bombay with two of his friends,
whom he now remembers only as Chopra and Suri, both probably Punjabis.[19] (Either Pahwa's memory was failing or he was
distancing himself from his activities during Partition. Except
for Nathuram and Gopal Godse, Pahwa could not remember the
full name of anyone he talked about. For the sake of the histori-
cally minded, I have supplied the first names of some of the better
known figures who make an appearance in his story.)

In Bombay, the three friends stayed at a refugee camp in
Chembur and began to kill Muslims on the streets of the city.
Bakshi asked him at this point wherefrom and how he got his
weapons, the bullets for instance. A lot of weapons were then
available in Bombay, Pahwa said, but did not name the suppliers
and procurers. Nor did he mention his own work as a clandestine
producer and seller of hand grenades, in high demand at the time.
It was while working in his illegal factory that the index finger of
his left hand got caught in a machine and, fearful that his activities
would become public, he picked up a knife and chopped the top
of the finger instead of calling a doctor.[20]

Something of the school bully had persisted in him and taken
a grotesque form in the wake of Partition. The Muslims were
no longer a predominantly friendly people whom he would
remember in his old age with fondness and nostalgia. They had

[19] Both names are Punjabi and it is probable that they too were refugees or
from families that had suffered directly or indirectly from the Partition.
[20] Madanlal Pahwa to Malgonkar, *The Men Who Killed Gandhi*, pp. 69–70.

become a monolithic monster against whom indiscriminate violence was justified. Pahwa went on to describe nonchalantly the petty thuggery that accompanied his peculiar mix of politics, violence, revenge, and relief:

> We would go into an Irani hotel, eat lots of food and then refuse to pay and leave. We also collected money and gave to refugees in the Chembur camp. We learnt of a Hindu girl from Lahore who had been brought here [Bombay] by a Muslim. ... We went and freed her.

In course of time, Pahwa started a business in fruits in Bombay. This sometimes took him to Ahmednagar where he bought some of his supplies. There he met Vishnu Karkare and they became friends. (The other version of the story is that Karkare, who had come to Ahmednagar to look for a reliable source of hand grenades, met Madanlal.)[21] Like Parchure, Karkare, too, was to join the conspiracy to kill Gandhi and was later tried and convicted. Karkare challenged Pahwa to throw a bomb in a cinema, implying that Pahwa would not have the guts to do so. 'I did it. I got the bomb from army people who had stolen it. There were lots of weapons like this available. The bomb killed between 15 and 20 persons in the cinema.'

Rajni Bakshi—she later said in a candid letter to me—was shocked and at a loss for words. She could only ask: 'How many of these people were Hindus and how many Muslims?' Pahwa did not know and did not care: 'It didn't matter; it was just a dare from Karkare.' Bakshi persisted nonetheless: 'Gandhi was a specific target, an enemy. But these common people were innocent. How do you justify this?'

'They were not innocent', Pahwa replied.

—'How and why?'

—'There mostly the scoundrels went to the cinema.'

[21] Ibid.

—'But how do you justify this, having said that you are a humanist?

—'I am that way *now*. At that time, it was right to throw the bomb.'

The exchange did not cramp Pahwa's style. He went on to tell the interviewer how, when violence broke out in Hyderabad, he and his friends moved there.

—'What did you do there?'

—'More killings. What else? They were robbing our villages, we robbed theirs.'

Madanlal seemed determined to not see the contradiction between what he had done to innocent Muslims far removed from the theatres of war in north and east India and what he had earlier said about Muslims being a friendly people laid astray by some ill-motivated Muslim politicians.

The interview flagged after this, Bakshi admits. She was a Gandhian but confronting in real life what some may call sickness of soul, she felt morally outraged and disoriented. She was not a clinician and the protection of clinical distance was not available to her. She wrote to me, 'At that point, I admit and confess that I lost interest in the interview. I just could not think of another thing to ask him. No, I did not actually feel claustrophobic, but I was happy to leave soon after.'[22] She also revealed that she felt being tested by me through these interviews.

ॐ

After he returned from Hyderabad, Pahwa was sucked into the conspiracy to kill Gandhi. The assassination was planned after Gandhi insisted that India 'give away' the Rs 550 million due to Pakistan as part of the Partition settlement.

[22] Rajni Bakshi to Ashis Nandy, 15 September 1999.

The original plan was for Digambar Badge, who used to supply arms to Pahwa and his associates, to shoot Gandhi; the bomb Pahwa planted at Gandhi's prayer meeting was meant as a distraction. But Badge ran away; he was to later turn an approver in the Gandhi murder trial. Pahwa was caught because, after entering the gate and studying the place for a while, he decided where to place the bomb. A woman and her child were sitting close by, so he told her to move because a bomb was about to go off. This woman, Sulochana Devi, informed the police and he was caught right away.[23] Karkare, Apte, and Nathuram then worked out another plan.

Bakshi tried to find out the involvement of the RSS and Hindu Mahasabha in the conspiracy—for long a subject of political debate. Pahwa responded in general terms but with reasonable candour: 'A party would never assist such a venture; such jobs only the brave do. A party always protects itself.' He flaunted his heroism in other ways too. He claimed that he did not reveal anything after his arrest, despite police torture. However, other sources say that he sang like a canary and gave the police vital details like the names and occupations of some of the conspirators. The police even traced the letters Pahwa exchanged with his girlfriend Shevanta at Bombay.[24] On 30 January 1948, he was lying on a block of ice when the police told him that Gandhi had been assassinated. One of the policemen said, 'You killed him finally.' Pahwa's response was: 'Good that the bastard has died; our troubles have ended (*achchā huā mar gayā sālā, hamāri museebat khatm hui*).' Bakshi interjected: 'Millions of people all over

---

[23] This action seems incongruent with Pahwa's days at Bombay, Gwalior, and Hyderabad, particularly his casual attitude to human life. His own descriptions of his career as a killer could be exaggerated. On the other hand, police records and Malgonkar's work support Pahwa's stories.

[24] Malgonkar, *The Men Who Killed Gandhi*, p. 73.

the world mourned Gandhi's death. How did you feel about that?'
The refugee from Pakpattan was unrepentant: 'The more people
were unhappy, the happier we were. ... Gandhi sired the Hindu-
Muslim ideology and he was the Father of Pakistan.'

Bakshi asked if he had any second thoughts on the murder?
'There has been none,' Pahwa claimed. There were, he said, two
turning points in his attitude to Gandhi. The first was the exit
of Subhas Chandra Bose from the Congress party. 'Till 1934 or
1936, I thought well of Gandhi. But when Bose was sacked as
the President of the Congress party and expelled from it, we gave
up.' According to Pahwa, Mohammad Ali Jinnah was the best
Congressman. When Jinnah saw more importance and power
being given to Mohammed and Shaukat Ali, he turned away from
the Congress party. The second turning point was the communal violence that broke out in 1946: 'Noakhali was the starting
point of all the violence. The worst violence was after 1946. There
was violence before that but it was not so bad.' Pahwa's use of
these two events to justify his politics tells one more about him
than about those he talked about. First, the Congress session
where Bose resigned took place in early 1939. Pahwa might have
admired Gandhi while growing up in Pakpattan, but it is unlikely
that as a child of 11, he had heard about the politics of that resig-
nation. It was probably an afterthought. Second, the violence of
Partition did not begin in Noakhali but in Calcutta on 14 August
1946. Pahwa remembers Noakhali because only Hindus were the
victims there; in Calcutta the victims were Hindus and Muslims.

More important, fifty years after the event, Gandhi seemed
to dominate Pahwa's world. Pahwa still desperately needed him,
as a larger-than-life figure of authority—an unacceptable moral
authority that had to be defied at every opportunity and
re-assassinated—to give meaning to his life. Pahwa must have been
especially pleased to meet his Gandhian interlocutor, one of the

few persons of the younger generation to whose self-definition Gandhi was central. Convincing Bakshi could be the next best thing to convincing Gandhi himself of the genuineness of the cause for which Pahwa had fought, killed, and suffered.

During the exchange, Bakshi asked, 'How was Gandhi alone, or even primarily, responsible for Pakistan?' Pahwa's response was revealing: 'Because the others were only nominally there.' Gandhi was the prime mover in Indian politics and selecting him as the enemy was the ultimate defiance of authority and the moral universe associated with that authority. Even when Bakshi rejected Pahwa's politics and values, unlike many others of her generation, she did not live in a post-Gandhian India, where both Gandhi and his assassins belonged to history. She lived in a world infused with Gandhi and was, thus, a perfect target, symbol of a rejected authority, standing witness to Pahwa's defiance and his attempts to shock through irreverent, amoral, provocative comments. The two had more to share than either could admit.

At the same time, despite tough talk, a part of Pahwa sought acceptance, almost pathetically, not merely from Bakshi but from Gandhi himself. Pahwa complained of rejection and partiality like a child feeling wronged by a father, unwilling to listen to his children under the influence of a hostile stepmother. The assassination was something that *had* to be done, for there was no other way ['*majbooran karnā padā*']. Nathuram Godse had bowed down to show respect to Gandhi before shooting him and had later told Gandhi's son Devdas that he had not dishonoured Gandhi but given him a hero's death. Pahwa was supplying a cruder version of the same self-justification.

That man [Gandhi] just would not listen [*veh ādmi suntā hi nahin thā*]. He gifted a Mahatma to the Muslims, nothing to the Hindus. Otherwise, he could have been a good leader. He wanted to be a *pir* of the Muslims, but did not succeed.

Godse in his last testament in the court accused Gandhi of failing in his paternal duty as the father of the nation and betraying Mother India. Pahwa's no less oedipal accusation was that Gandhi was not an impartial father. Pahwa had to be more bitter in his self-justification; he held Gandhi responsible even for the hanging of freedom fighter Bhagat Singh by the colonial regime and claimed that Gandhi had sent a telegram to Shah Amanullah to attack India and restore Muslim rule.[25]

✵

The way he put together his story, one suspects that Pahwa had walked a monotonous, anti-climactic life after coming out of jail. Indeed, he had faithfully followed the advice of the only one in the assassination team for whom he had genuine warmth, Nathuram Godse. He was not in touch with serious politics after his release and Indian politics also had passed him by. Contemporary politics did not enter his narrative, even though his ideology had become more salient in India during the previous two decades. His was the story of a person trying to re-enter life as a householder after a life-altering 'heroic' experience. The only politics that mattered to him was the politics of the 1940s and, psychologically, he had continued to live in that decade. When interviewed, he was suffering from a kidney ailment for about seven years. That too he had to relate to his pivotal experience; it was, he claimed, 'due to the torture in 1948'.

After his release in 1964, Pahwa first went to his father in Gurgaon and then to Poona to join Gopal Godse. For a while, he worked as a salesman for a company dealing with automobile

---

[25] Pahwa here was alluding to the fact that Gandhi did not make the commutation of the death sentence on Bhagat Singh a political issue. The telegram, of course, was a concoction.

parts but, when they came to know his past, they threw him out. Then, one M.H. Vyas, an advocate and a Hindu Mahasabha leader, gave him a place to stay in Bombay. Pahwa did a series of odd jobs and was, towards the end of his active life, the Secretary of Bombay Hotel Owners Association. He ran an employment agency when he was interviewed.

In 1966, Pahwa got married to Damayanti in Bombay. The marriage was arranged by Gopal Godse, who persuaded Damayanti and her parents. No relative from Pahwa's side came for the marriage. Pahwa's relationship with his family, strained since his childhood, was by now even more tenuous. Damayanti, a Maharashtrian, seemed a devoted wife. When Rajni Bakshi asked her what she thought of his past, Damayanti said, 'He did it for the country, not for personal reasons.' Some might have been suspicious of that formulaic statement, but Damayanti probably had lived with that explanation for decades.[26]

Did he have any regrets, any repentance, Bakshi asked at the end? 'None', said Madanlal Pahwa, but quickly qualified the statement. 'What I did then was right in those circumstances. What I think and do now is right in today's circumstances.' Did that assertion hide some deeper discomfort? Did he imply that his actions would have been immoral in other circumstances? He did say at one point, 'We Indians are humanists but, when required, we can kill, too.'

I have said that, while Pahwa had remained outside politics, the meaning to his otherwise bland life was given by a political

---

[26] We know from Malgonkar's account that before going to jail, while at Bombay, Pahwa had acquired a girlfriend. After his arrest the police recovered a couple of her passionate, erotically tinged love letters to him. The letters were used by the prosecution in the court. Apart from these, we know nothing about their writer except her name, Shevanta. She has, at some point of time, slipped out of the pages of history. Malgonkar, pp. 73–4.

act that he had to repeatedly and compulsively revisit in his
memories. Like many others of his ideological persuasion,
he was still immersed in the politics of the 1940s—the short-
sightedness of the Congress party under Gandhi; appeasement
of Muslims, particularly Muslim fundamentalists, by the likes of
Gandhi and Nehru; and the suffering of the Hindus affected by
the division of British India. These were the main themes in his
story. Time had stopped for him at the time of Partition and the
moment of Gandhi's death. Pahwa's definition of fanaticism
was also distinctive. It allowed him to claim that he was once
a fanatic but had since become a humanist. When Bakshi asked
him what he meant by 'fanatic', he said,

> The fanatic ... sees only the flaws in others and turns against them.
> This is what happened to the Hindus and the Muslims at the time
> of Partition. Fanaticism blinds a person. But *insāniyat*, humanity, is
> also there. I have trust in humanity. In this world, no one is born evil.
> Circumstances make a person bad.

It was as if Pahwa was defending himself. 'If a Hindu girl is
assaulted, then, for a moment, fanaticism takes over'—'*junoon ho
jātā hai.*'

I have already mentioned the distance between Pahwa and
his family, particularly his father, whom he seemed to consider
a harsh, demanding authority, unable to protect his son from an
aggressive stepmother. However, Pahwa's relationship with most
of his associates too was shallow. As we have seen, he could not
remember the full names of most of them, even when they were
well-known figures. There had been only two strong emotional
bonds in his remembered life. He was tied to Gandhi through
hatred, to Godse through affection. Godse was the only one for
whom Pahwa admitted crying. Godse in turn was fond of Pahwa,
at 20 the youngest of the conspirators. Godse would point out to

young Madanlal the love-play of birds from the prison cell and say: 'Look, now you too fall in love. You have done enough for the country.'

Pahwa remembered that on the day of the execution of Godse and Apte, they all got up and had coffee together at 5 a.m. prior to the hanging at 7 a.m., Nathuram especially wanted to talk to Madanlal. 'Don't cry; I am about to become a martyr,' Godse said. He then advised Pahwa to get married. His last words to Pahwa were: 'We have done our work, now don't bother about politics.' Pahwa's account reconfirms what seems to emerge from a number of other works, that the plot to kill Gandhi was held together by the personality of Godse—his simple dignity, austere life, ideological commitment, and perhaps also the distinctive amalgam of fear, hatred, and respect for Gandhi. Pahwa's self-definition was a warped reflection of the same mix.

ಎರಿ

Ideology versus Roots

This is a case of a perpetrator who justifies and yet distances himself from his past. Pahwa might have been violent even as a teenager but he had no prior criminal record. He was a young man driven by two emotions: revenge—and a distorted idea of resistance linked to it—and a less conspicuous but desperate attempt to redeem self-esteem, individual and collective. Like thousands of other ordinary citizens, he too was pushed into the vortex of violence by his passion. Ideology did enter the picture as a legitimizing principle, for while Pahwa had turned an accomplished killer before joining the plot to kill Gandhi, we cannot be sure if his ideology freed him from his inner restraints or justified his killings ex post facto.

In decentralized forms of mass violence, what Mamdani has in mind when he talks of 'popular genocide', the feelings and motivations of the killers matter, for they are ordinary people to whom killing does not come easy. Without the right mix of these feelings and motives, the killers cannot be mobilized for genocidal purposes, for there is no centralized killing machine. The violence of 1946–8 was mostly an anarchic affair. But it had pockets of planned, organized, fragmented but dedicated cadre chains, and packaged political ideologies and categories to sanction the killings, abductions, rapes, arson, and pillage. The violence did not happen; it was made to happen.

Because Partition violence was mainly a decentralized venture, one must explore the inner dynamics that helped breach self-restraint and seduced ordinary citizens into mobs or vigilante groups and made homicide imaginable from within the confines of everyday life. Both Veena Das and Sudhir Kakar talk of the transient heroic stature that otherwise insignificant persons, often living at the margins of law and society, can acquire as defenders of a community and its honour.[27] The opportunities for such status gain widen when there is, as was in India during 1946–8, not only a collapse of political authority but also an apparent suspension of traditional codes of conduct—a weird combination of *matsyanyaya* and a crypto-Hobbesian state of nature, brought about by the massive withdrawal of the British-Indian state from governance.[28]

---

[27] Veena Das, *Critical Events: An Anthropological Perspective on Contemporary India* (New Delhi: Oxford University Press, 1995); Sudhir Kakar, *The Colours of Violence: Cultural Identities, Religion, and Conflict* (New Delhi: Oxford University Press, 1996), see Ch. on 'The Warriors'.

[28] The only serious effort to capture the state of governance in British India in those days is Stanley Wolpert, *Shameful Flight: The Last Years of British Empire in India* (New York: Oxford University Press, 2006).

With the once-awe-inspiring authorities in stupor, there could not but be moments when meting out 'justice'—by giving or taking life—gave to many perpetrators a sense of omnipotence. What would have been simple greed or revenge got redeemed as 'moral' moments in amoral times.

Religious nationalism enters the picture through this psychological crevice, not through the institutional pathway global common sense maps out. Pahwa dutifully projects his Hindu nationalism even into his childhood but cannot sustain the ideological thrust of his story. His narrative—in essence a simple tale of neighbourliness and shared spirituality, followed by uncontrolled rage at a paradise lost and the consequent hunger for revenge—rebels against the intrusion. His attempt to disown his earlier hooligan self and to portray himself as a humanist in his advanced years can also be read as an attempt to make peace with and defend his childhood memories, organized around a lifestyle in which the Hindus and Muslims might not have been in a permanent fraternal embrace but were indispensable to each other as communities collaboratively defining the meaning of everyday life.[29] In his new, uneasy incarnation as a humanist, Pahwa could not but return to the idea of a 'normal' Muslim—friendly, cultivated, and sharing even religious space with the Hindus. To do so, he has to set up a subset of violent, anti-Hindu Muslims, led astray by conspiratorial politicians.

Pahwa's story has another key component. It recognizes but recoils from the idea that targeting the Muslims indiscriminately was his way of targeting authority figures nearer home and the moral universe they represented. Once the opportunities for such

---

[29] Cf. Ashis Nandy, 'Time Travels to a Possible Self: Searching for the Alternative Cosmopolitanism of Cochin', *Time Warps: The Insistent Politics of Silent and Evasive Pasts* (New Delhi: Permanent Black, London: C. Hurst and Co., New York: Rutgers University Press, 2002), pp. 157–209.

defiance opened up, Pahwa's inner checks failed. The rejection of Gandhi, as an extension of authoritative source of morality, smoothened this transition.

Like many others we have interviewed, Pahwa is burdened by prejudices and stereotypes against Muslims, yet, they are nearer to him as interpersonal realities. He has lived in a Muslim-majority society and has had close Muslim friends. He has entry into their world and even into the domain of spirituality identified with Islam. He cannot but oscillate between perceptions of Muslims as an undifferentiated mass and Muslims as a diverse community in which some thugs spout a violent ideology. Pahwa is not hostile to strangers but to neighbours who have turned strangers.

That is perhaps why, as in some other victims and perpetrators from rural Punjab, Hindu nationalism did not have a total hold on Pahwa. That did not soften his violence, with its clear psychopathic tinge—he took out his anger against the southern and western Indian Muslims for what had befallen the northern and eastern Indian Hindus. From an urban hoodlum illegally producing and selling arms and making a living out of small-time thuggery, he rose to briefly become a significant political actor and an agent of 'history.' His ideological posture and ultra-nationalist rhetoric bore the stamp of downmarket Bombay, Hyderabad, and the smaller cities of the erstwhile Bombay state; they were parts of a first-generation migrant's attempt to find psychological space in a city.

ॐ

Though we have said at the beginning that the killers in the violence of 1946–8 went scot-free, that is not the whole story. A 'popular' genocide can have an unpopular underside, even for those who participate in it. They, too, have to pay a price. The price may not be commensurate with the crime, but it is not trivial either. Pahwa *was* cramped by his past and permanently yoked to his memories; he had to constantly try to retrace his steps, even while saying that he had no reason to do so. Over a period of six decades, he had erected a usable set of defences and also worked out his answers to his detractors. He continued to flaunt his homicidal record as a badge of honour, a record of what he has done for the health and longevity of the young Indian nation-state. But the defences were still not strong enough; they could not fully answer Pahwa's own questions.

Behind his bravado and practised rhetoric lurked an unsure Pakpattan boy seeking acceptance from a world that had rejected him. He could neither disown the past that gave meaning to his life nor live with it in peace. His doubling was a way of making peace with his personal memories of a violent, partial father through Hindu nationalism's 'screen history' of India and the role in that history of the man he conspired to kill as a false paternal authority. The preoccupation with Gandhi—and the pitiable effort to find justification from values that might have been acceptable to his famous victim—were also an attempt to return to a self predating the one event that anchored his life.

That earlier self to which Pahwa sought to return was the one I identified at the beginning as the non-canonical, local, vernacular stratum of popular religion. The memories associated with Baba Fareed's mazār, the fulcrum of Pahwa's earlier self, could not but be a negation of his ideological self.

ఌ

This story can be read as a case study of a heartless killer sentenced to life imprisonment, not for killing Muslims but for killing Gandhi for his bias towards the Muslims. Had Pahwa not been part of the conspiracy, he would have gone scot-free. Yet, that impunity was not conclusive. As he in his advanced years moved diffidently towards the vernacular tradition of religion he was reared on and towards its distinctive forms of openness and inclusivity, he was bound to become a bundle of contradictions and unwittingly tilt towards a worldview where the Muslims and Islam had a place and so had even Gandhi. The border-lines between faiths had once again become porous for Pahwa. Despite all efforts to remain loyal to his ideology—including its Europeanized ideas of religion, state, and nation—Pahwa had become a bundle of contradictions. His Hindutva had failed to defend him from the vernacular Hinduism and Islam of his ancestral village intruding into his world. Which past was Pahwa's own? Pahwa himself probably did not know. He could neither disown his ideology nor Pakpattan.

Have I told the story of a person battling memories of loss and exile through violence, or is it the story of a killer representing the anomic violence Partition unleashed? I am afraid, I must leave the readers with the question, hoping that they can find an answer for me.

R eturn of the Sacred

Politics of Religion in a Post-secular Age

I cannot now remember when exactly I lost and, then, was forced to rediscover religion. But I know that the loss was triggered by the sudden expansion of my world through an encounter with the sceptical, secular, intellectual culture of mid-twentieth-century Calcutta in my teens. Perhaps the spirit of youthful rebellion against authorities also had something to do with it; my parents were devout believers. The rediscovery, when it came after about thirty-five years, was slow and mainly a cognitive venture, not precipitated by any personal crisis, newfound spiritual sentiments or faith, but by a concern with the career and fate of democracy all over the globe, especially in that part of it that nowadays goes by the name of the South. The rediscovery was to acquire other emotional and political associations later, but those

are not particularly relevant to our concerns here. As I look back
at my life, however, one thing is pretty clear to me. Faith cannot
be reclaimed as the end product of a cognitive venture. You can,
at most, acquire some respect for those who hold or live by faiths
and grant the presence of some sacredness in selected areas of
human affairs—perhaps to give some sanctity to human and non-
human life, nature, and childhood, and to ideas like androgyny
and reproduction.

✑

For reasons I have not yet fully grasped, the political geography
of both religion and democracy began to change after World
War II and the changes began to become more apparent during
the 1970s and 1980s. At least to me. And I could be considered
an interested spectator and a product of those times.

First, suddenly the number of democracies in the world
grew from about a dozen to more than hundred and the world
population living under democracy quadrupled. Most of these
were newly independent countries and it soon became obvious
that in many of these new democracies, sizeable sections of the
citizens were exercising their democratic rights not to advance
their individual needs or demands, but to push their collective cultural, religious, or communal demands. Such demands
were always there in democracies but, in the older democracies,
the demands had become more predictable, manageable and,
when not so, they were usually the demands of small vocifer-
ous minorities, often dismissed as a lunatic fringe or as harmless eccentrics. In the new democracies, on the other hand, these
demands often looked strange, dangerous, unpredictable, and
primordial. The borderlines among culture, religion, and community looked blurred and the domains seemed to run into

one another. The demands naturally aroused widespread anxiety and fear in the older democracies and among the first-generation ruling elite in Asia and Africa.

Secondly and simultaneously, there grew the fear of what the newly enfranchised citizens in the new democracies were bringing into politics by way of cultural preferences. These included new styles and values in governance, indeed new protocols of democracy. These protocols often encompassed new styles of nepotism and corruption, new forms of reverence and irreverence, and new hierarchies of ideological and non-ideological commitments. In these too, there was the tacit presence of religion. In the sense that political actors often seemed terribly under-socialized in existing patterns of expectation from democratic politics, the law and order machinery, and a secular state. Often they lifted public values and cognitive frames straight from their diverse religious worldviews.

Third, democracy may or may not succeed in distributing economic and social power, but it always redistributes charisma. Indeed, democracy can and perhaps should be redefined as an institutionalized means of decentralizing and redistributing charisma. In even a flawed democracy, charisma tends to be unstable and labile; frequently it refuses to remain concentrated in designated persons or institutions; it has a permanent long-term, secular tendency to get redistributed and expand the chances of the citizens to share the charisma that once was more centralized. I have in mind not merely the way terms like 'people', masses, and citizens acquired potency in politics—they actually began to do so quite early in the career of democracy, in the late nineteenth century—but also how the invisible wall of respect and awe around the rulers now have begun to show signs of fragility.

This redistribution affects everyone living in a democracy. The way President John F. Kennedy's sexual escapades were treated by

the media and the American public was not the way President
Bill Clinton's were treated. Likewise, the discretion with which
President Mitterrand's illegitimate daughter was allowed to
become public knowledge towards the end of his life has not been
evident in the case of President Nicolas Sarkozy's sexual life. The
charisma attaching to presidency, it can be argued, is differently
and perhaps more thinly concentrated in the person of president
in both countries now.

Even when charisma is heavily concentrated in non-traditional
domains, such as cinema stars and sports persons, it is mostly transient, with no institutional attempt to legitimize it, no grand social
or political theory, and certainly no theology. In the domain of
religions too, in parts of the world, while the importance of char-
ismatic religious leaders and evangelists have grown, the Church
paradoxically no longer looks that awe-inspiring and exclusive
and the non-Christian religions not so irreligious. Old-style
evangelism may be flourishing, but new forms of self-induced
conversion or choosing another religion in addition to one's own,
without actually converting, is also becoming more common. This
expansion of religious choice—it includes smaller choices that
cut across religious lines, such as the growing popularity of yoga,
Tibetan healing traditions, and Christian marriage rituals among
non-Christian communities—has made many religious leaders
and defenders of faith nervous and doubly defensive. They suspect
they are living in a new, uncertain, strange world, and they sometimes try to cope with their fears through cognitive closure. The
same fears and the same closure can be seen among those allegiant
to the new substitutes for religion of our times, nationalism and
secularism. In Turkey, France, and India, for instance, any inter-
rogation of such faiths is seen as virtually unnatural act.

Fourth, it has become obvious that in the South the encounter with aggressively evangelical Christianity during the colonial

times has produced among some of the major faiths a reaction that psychoanalysts will call identification with the aggressor—an attempt to produce from within their ranks revised versions of the faith that can stand up to the evangelical challenge of masculine, Protestant Christianity by being like it. These attempts have been fired by the conviction that this particular form of religion was more compatible with modernity, national state, and industrial capitalism. In South Asia, for instance, both Hinduism and Buddhism, though considered ancient faiths, have produced their own versions of Protestant reform movements such as Brahmo Samaj (founded in 1830), Arya Samaj (1875), Ramakrishna Mission (1897), and Mahabodhi Society (1891), and reformers such as Rammohun Roy (1772–1822), Dayananda Saraswati (1824–1883), Swami Vivekananda (1863–1902), and Anagarika Dharmapala (1864–1933). Only small groups of people have actually opted for belief systems these movements propagated, but they have changed the entire culture of religion in the region. To this extent, Hinduism and Buddhism as we know them today in urban, middle-class South Asia are all new faiths, not much more than a century old. (For the moment, I am not discussing the case of South Asian Islam because similar movements in Islam acquired momentum later and their influence became obvious even later. One should be able to say Islam, too, is becoming a new faith today.)

The most important, common core of these projects has been a two-fold attempt to brush up the faiths. The more overt part of the effort has been to make them more compatible with modern rationality and scientific spirit; cleanse them of the 'superstitions', 'meaningless' rituals and local customs that have come to be associated with them; and determined attempts to give their theology—and their 'philosophical' beliefs—a higher status than their rituals, rites, and practices. The more covert goals were to use these means to centralize the faiths, give them well-charted borders, and make them more compatible, manageable, and subservient to the demands of a modern nation-state and its ideas of secularism and the needs of a modern, urban-industrial society.

Responding to these processes and occasionally rebelling against them, there have been attempts to re-imagine the relationship between politics and religion and open a more self-confident, open-ended dialogue between them during the last five decades. We all know of such initiatives and all I have to do here is to mention, as examples, three of them that have been prominent. First, religion has re-emerged as an epic of the oppressed and as a language of resistance. Liberation theology in Christianity and Ali Shariati in Islam are reasonably good examples. I said re-emerged, not emerged, because this is a use of religion known to all religions since ancient times. It has been rediscovered because the fond nineteenth-century belief that this-worldly, science-based, secular knowledge will supply theories of liberation more appropriate for our times lies shattered and discredited all around us. At the same time, with the decline of the secular power of organized religion, the priestly classes no longer look so formidable, despite the return and spread of fundamentalism in many parts of the world.

Second, the spreading belief that the processes of disenchantment and desacralization have gone too far has led to determined efforts to reclaim some areas of life from what look like the clutches of the secular, for purposes of resacralization. Some of the most conspicuous of these areas are environment, reproductivity (as an antipode or negation of productivity), childhood, and life itself.

Third, the major South Asian faiths do not have centralized, overarching, church-like structures that can be engaged, appeased, or bargained with. This has led to the emergence of new kinds of political formations that try to act like brokers between the state and highly diverse religious communities, but have no intrinsic sanction in the community to do so. They enjoy political support, mainly among the urban, educated, modernized or semi-modernized middle classes that have moved towards an idea of religion as a standardized, generic, global belief-system. These formations can also act as political pressure groups in a democratic order and begin to influence public policy under certain circumstances.

There are other important processes at work too. But the ones I have mentioned have most influenced my work on religion and politics, particularly my critique of secularism and my fascination with Mohandas Karamchand Gandhi's maxim that it is impossible to imagine politics without religion. The rest of this essay is a brief introduction to my position on the subject.

ငာ

No one thought that religion would re-emerge from the shadows to occupy centre-stage at the beginning of the twenty-first century. Many wrote obituaries of religions as early as in the middle of the nineteenth century. Since then, it has been the triumph of one secular ideology after another, though steep decline or ignominious fall has usually followed the triumph. Religion has re-emerged at the end of what could be called an age of ideologies, not in its pristine form but bearing the imprint and, sometimes, even the garb of the age of secular ideologies. At the beginning of the twenty-first century, religion is a phoenix that has risen from its own ashes and wears the ashes as a sign of its new triumph.

This may or may not be an enigma. The attempts to banish all mystery and spirituality from life, the increasing poverty of the individualism that envelops lonely crowds in fully developed consumer societies, the steady growth of violence, often gratuitous, the decline in the sanctity of life that finds expression not only in wars, machine violence, and torture but also in assaults on the environment and the life-support system of the coming generations, widespread use of the Enlightenment values and secular state-craft as justifications for new forms of dominance and despotism—they all have contributed to the erosion of the easy faith in the age of reason and the unlimited power of human reason.[1]

At the same time, the religious worldview is a worldview after all and like all other worldviews it too carries a baggage. After the crusades and holy wars, the genocide of indigenous peoples in the Americas, slavery and colonialism sanctioned by powerful sections of the Christian church, and the more recent rise in religion-based terrorism in the Islamic world, and the blatant secular use of religion in South Asian politics—where Hinduism, Islam, Buddhism, and Sikhism have been periodically used to mobilize hatred—we are left with no alternative but to admit that the world of religion parallels the secular world and can be as much a domain of gratuitous violence, paranoia, and sadomasochism. It is true that one look at R.J. Rummel's data and some rough arithmetical manipulation of them reveal that in the last hundred years fully secular states have killed at least forty-five times as many people as religious violence and fundamentalism have killed.[2] But then, as Charles Long likes to say, 'secularism is a

---

[1] See, for instance, Alister McGrath, *The Twilight of Atheism: The Rise and Fall of Disbelief in the Modern World* (New York: Doubleday, 2004). An instance of the growing doubts about the efficacy of secularism within political theory is William E. Connolly, *Why I am not a Secularist* (Minneapolis: University of Minnesota, 1999).

[2] R.J. Rummel, *Death by Government: Genocide and Mass Murder Since 1900* (West Hanover, Mass.: Christopher Publishing, 1994).

hidden religion for which no one has to take any responsibility.' It is probably safer to presume that given opportunities, people will kill, rape, and plunder in the name of religion as happily as people have done in the name of secular statecraft, nationalism, progress, revolution, and development.

Only two things have changed. First, whatever may have happened in the past, the violence that religion *now* sanctions cannot compete in range and depth with the violence that modern states routinely sanction in the name of secular ideologies and nationalism. Second, being primarily interest-based and a pathology of rationality, state violence has increasingly become more organized, scientific, efficient, and user-friendly, whereas religious violence, to the extent it is passion-based and a pathology of irrationality, still leaves more scope for individual and collective resistance, by having some loopholes and sectors of inefficiency. I hasten to add, however, that these differences are getting smudged; in its new incarnation, religious violence too is acquiring many of the features of state violence.

ଏଓ

Why should then we negotiate the domain of religion as citizens? Why should we learn the language of religion or enter the cosmology of religion? The honest answer is that we do not have to, except as ethnographers, historians, or psychologists. At one time it must have been different, but now millions of people live without the benefit of faith. It is unlikely that one would run out of company if one refuses to learn the language or enter the cosmology of religion. One can easily converse with a sizeable number of people in the academe, in professions, and in the higher echelons of the state who speak the language of secular statecraft and individual citizenship.

However, an even larger part of the world and a huge majority of those staying in the godforsaken parts of the world—in Latin America, Africa, and Asia—have partial or no access to the language of secularism and citizenship. Often they have been denied such citizenship, though invited to use the language of citizenship. Anyone who refuses to learn the language and the cosmology of religion has, as a result, little or no access to that other world. This is no great loss if you are a modern academic in a modern university, or if you plan to live exclusively within the confines of one of the many pockets of modernity that pock-mark the southern hemisphere. I am fully aware that mostly the poor, the marginal, the retrogressive, and the disposable today seem to have religion. However, if you happen to be one of those who take democratic participation seriously or seek to influence public life and public policy in the Southern world, it becomes a different story.

This is because, without some access to the religious world-view, you will pretty soon become primarily a spectator of politics and left with only the option of constantly bemoaning the bad choices that 'ignorant', 'ill-informed', 'irrational' electorates make and shedding copious tears on the rise of religious funda-mentalism and ethnic chauvinism encouraged by competitive democracy. You will also have to, I am afraid, reconcile yourself to lamenting the way the ungodly and the ill-motivated occupy increasingly larger public space just because they speak the lan-guage of religion and can converse from within a religious world-view. If you are enterprising enough, you might console yourself by writing angry columns in newspapers, or letters to editors, or talk of the good old days when politics and politicians were reportedly purer and more idealistic.

This is not a convoluted plea to return to faith or to estab-lish the superiority of the language of religion. It is a plea to acknowledge the costs of democracy. It presumes that in a democracy citizens have the right to bring their ethical frameworks within politics and the frameworks may not meet the criteria set up by their well-wishers. No sloganeering on the need to keep separate religion and politics—the church and the state—can work on those whose everyday ethics are directly or indirectly derived from religion, especially since we may not be able to employ a thought police efficient enough to force citizens to maintain such separation.[3] It is a pity, I am sure, that despite more than 300 years of spirited, dedicated efforts, so many still use religious cosmology as a ballast in life, particularly when buffeted by the disorienting pace of social change, uprooting, or personal insecurity. Many of us may not need such a ballast, but we cannot ensure that in a democracy others would not. The situation has been complicated in recent decades by the growing trend in many secular, modern states to set up as a political ploy, entire religions and civilizations as demonic others that need to be de-fanged. Those at the receiving end of such stereotypy are naturally finding it increasingly difficult to adore the secular worldview as intrinsically opposed to fanaticism and hatred.[4]

---

[3] For that matter, there is little evidence in contemporary psychology that people can maintain such separation within themselves on a long-term basis. Indeed, there is much evidence that they try to reduce such dissonance. While there is some evidence that South Asians can live with greater cognitive dissonance within themselves, this capacity is in decline in the urban melting pots of the region, where most religious violence takes place.

[4] On this subject, see for instance, Asma Barlas, 'The Secular Commitment to "Islamic Fundamentalism"', Daily Times, 4 August 2002. Barlas says at one place, '... one could argue, for instance, that whereas in the West, modernity brought the benefits of capitalism, industrialization, and representative democracy, for most of the world, it brought colonization, slavery, economic ruin, militarization of politics, increased poverty, the extinction of indigenous people and cultural alienation. Similarly, the very secularism that freed

Here, the African Americans in the United States have a lesson to offer to Africa and Asia, particularly to the South Asian intellectuals tirelessly speaking of the virtues of secularism. No one can deny that Christianity was virtually imposed on the Black community. Their Christianity bears the mark of their suffering over two centuries. Nevertheless, they have made something out of that imposition that is distinctively theirs. Christianity in turn, I dare say, has been at its creative best when deployed as a theology of emancipation by the African Americans and African Africans. From Reverend Martin Luther King to Reverend Desmond Tutu, it has been the unfolding of the potentialities of an Asian faith that defy the European heritage of Christianity to supply a potent political philosophy of militant non-violence that has radically changed our ideas of political resistance and dissent. (This Christianity, conversing with the Hindu–Jain traditions through Gandhi, has also initiated a remarkable dialogue of faiths in our times outside the academe and outside the range of standardized formats of dialogue.) It has emancipated European Christianity from some of its core conventions and, more important, its historical baggage, the history that prompted Mohandas Gandhi to say that Christianity was a good religion before it went to Europe. I need hardly add that the Truth and Reconciliation Commission in South Africa was not a secular enterprise.

"man"—in the masculinist language of the Enlightenment—from the alleged tyranny of religion, also opened up to doubt people's sense of themselves as purposive moral agents in the world. Hence, what some embraced as freedom, others experienced as profound loss.' For a powerful, detailed treatment of the issue, see Ali Mazrui, ' "Progress": Illegitimate Child of Judeo-Christian Universalism and Western Ethnocentrism—A Third World Critique', in Bruce Mazlish and Leo Marx (eds), *Progress: Fact or Illusion* (Ann Arbor: University of Michigan, 1996), pp. 153–74. Strangely, such arguments, when made in the context of Islam, are more acceptable in academic circles in India than when made in the context of Hinduism.

Nor was it a sui generis brainwave of Tutu. It was squarely located in an ecumenical normative frame that cut across faiths and ideologies, beliefs and disbeliefs. The commission was a clear case of religion intruding into politics, in a way that Gandhi would have applauded. Like everyone else, I am aware and critical of some limitations of the commission, but these limitations do not detract from the daring ethical imagination that inspired it.[5]

There is another lesson for us from the African Americans. Through all their struggles, they never yielded ground to the religious fanatics, though there were small, identifiable groups within them pushing violence and extremism. Because the community's leadership never abandoned the domain of religion as irrelevant to the public sphere, some of the most creative inputs into their struggle for equality and dignity came from within their religious consciousness. Those who fought fanaticism and bigotry among them could make sense to others in the community because they shared the language of religion. I could give similar examples from Latin America, the Sandinistas being one of the most conspicuous among them. The Sandinista cabinet included a number of priests and was headed by one, and the movement they represented, whatever its other flaws, never lost touch with the religious self of their constituency. It is not true that all shades of Marxism have to embrace, with fundamentalist fervour, the secularist dogma.

In India, on the other hand, the first generation of post-Independence leaders was respectful towards but fearful of Gandhi and his 'intemperate' use of religion in politics. Some of them, to the delight of 'progressive' intellectuals, quickly shifted to a political idiom that could be called an insipid copy of social-democratic

[5] For a glimpse into Tutu's own way of looking at the commission, see Desmond Tutu, *No Future without Forgiveness* (London: Rider, 1999).

ideologies floating around in Europe, especially Fabian socialism of the inter-war years, leavened with a pinch of the hard materialism of the Leninist kind. They declared the entire domain of religion untouchable and left it to its 'natural' carriers—the 'backward', 'illiterate', 'provincial' apprentice-citizens of the society.[6]

The results of that short-sightedness and obeisance to transient fashions could only be disastrous, when combined with the latent fear and contempt for the ordinary citizens and their worldviews and categories. Taking advantage of this fear and contempt, small groups of Hindu, Muslim, Buddhist, and Sikh political activists have taken over the responsibility of speaking for these religions. Even the occasional attempts to deploy the language and cosmology of religion to counter extremism and violence enjoy little legitimacy because the credibility of anyone from the modern sector speaking on religious matters has been badly compromised.

The modern intelligentsia in India, too, has devalued the leadership of more serious religious leaders by mechanically accepting the credentials of the political activists speaking on behalf of religious communities. This intelligentsia has to take on face value everyone who claims to speak on behalf of a religion—from psychopathic, violence-prone, rabble-rousers trying to break into politics to scheming, paranoiac necrophiles among the political leaders—because it itself does not have any serious acquaintance with the world of religion. One of the saddest spectacles in India in recent years has been the effort of some Catholic religious figures to open a dialogue with the un-elected, self-proclaimed leaders of Hindus like the Rashtriya Swayamsevak Sangh (RSS)

---

[6] The fear of what religion might do is best illustrated by the absence of a single department of religious studies in any of India's roughly 300 universities, even though many of them are modelled on famous Western universities known for their departments of religious studies.

and the Vishwa Hindu Parishad (VHP), whose interest in the context of Hinduism has been close to zero. These are formations that claim to speak for all Hindus of the world—the one billion of them—when they and the parties they support have together never won even one-third of Hindu votes in India.

&

There is a built-in contradiction in the tenor of my argument here. I have made a case for understanding religious worldviews as means of entering popular consciousness and the normative frames that shape the democratic process and, sometimes, decide its fate. Yet, it remains an open question how far the worldviews directly shape democratic choices and how far they are mediated or altered by the packaged interpretations of religions floating around in the public sphere.[7]

On the other hand, believers are not obliged to believe in a manner acceptable to philosophers, theologians, and historians of religion. For many believers, religion is a matter of periodical participation in rituals and other modest observances. When we speak of the language of religion, do we have in mind what serious scholars and thinkers have in mind? Or do we have in mind the simple, everyday versions of the faith that look anti-philosophical and are often an embarrassment to sophisticated believers? Do we have in mind both? Perhaps the question is

---

[7] Elsewhere I have argued that most of these packaged software come not as religious cults or sects but as religion-based political ideologies that do not include any theory of transcendence. See for instance, Ashis Nandy, 'The Politics of Secularism and the Recovery of Religious Tolerance', in *Time Warps: The Insistent Politics of Silent and Evasive Pasts* (New Delhi: Permanent Black, 2002), pp. 61–88; and 'The Twilight of Certitudes: Secularism, Hindu Nationalism and Other Masks of Deculturation', in *The Romance of the State and the Fate Dissent in the Tropics* (New Delhi: Oxford University Press, 2003), pp. 61–82.

not that relevant, if the challenge is to bypass this division and discover the frames of sensitivity, the inter-subjectivity, within which the respect for—and celebration of—the unthinking, casual, everyday forms of religiosity also come to represent more serious visions of a sacralized cosmos and sanctity of life.

Though in my own work, when I use the term religion, I do not usually have in mind canonical texts or practices, the so-called high culture of religion, but the lowbrow and the non-canonical, contaminated by ordinary people and everyday life; I have not discussed here how the canonical and the high-cultural have gradually become the official and acquired the right to represent a religion. The modern state has always felt more comfortable with the classical and the canonical, for it has always a preference for the centralized and the well-organized as opposed to the decentralized and the chaotic.[8]

In South Asia, what was left undone by the colonial administrators, perpetually looking for a single, definitive version of a faith—so that the colonial states could cope with, manage, or arrive at a political quid pro quo with the native religions—was completed by the modern university system, ever eager to identify the 'real' form and core of a religion. Arab Islam became the definitive tradition of Islam only in the early part of the twentieth century, redefining the world's largest Islamic societies as abodes of peripheral Islam. *Manusamhita* became the final, authoritative text on Hindu law only in the middle of the nineteenth century, thanks to the efforts of the colonial dispensation to codify Hindu law. Over generations, these redefinitions have been internalized by large sections of modern, educated believers in

---

[8] Interested readers may like to look up Ashis Nandy, 'A Report on the Present State of Health of Gods and Goddesses in India', *Time Warps: The Insistent Politics of Silent and Evasive Pasts* (New Delhi: Permanent Black, 2002), pp. 129–56; and 'The Twilight of Certitudes'.

the Afro-Asian world. We are paying the costs of such central-
ization today. The pathetic effort of many Muslim communities
to defend their religious identity and self-esteem, by opting for
a blood-drenched version of 'pure' Islam, is only one part of the
story. For one sees a similar development in a number of other
religions, in which the axis of self-definition has shifted under
the onslaught of a new, 'universal' idea of faith popularized by the
nineteenth-century European knowledge system in general and
the European university system in particular.

Second, the religious worldview, being a worldview, always
has within it a place for irreverence, wit, and play. The global
triumph of European Protestantism during the nineteenth and
twentieth centuries, especially its close links with industrial
capitalism and colonialism and its ability to underwrite a house-
broken version of religion that is subservient to the nation-state,
has introduced or strengthened certain forms of Puritanism in
virtually every major religion. Some of the non-Semitic faiths,
bearing the imprint of the 'pagan' creeds have been particularly
unfortunate in this regard. A huge majority of their followers are
accustomed to some degree of playfulness, show of irreverent
familiarity, bargaining, blatant eroticism, and even accusations of
nepotism against divinities. However, a small minority, exposed
to the culture of religion in West Europe and North America, are
embarrassed by such disreputable behaviour and feel even more
offended if someone from outside the fold is audacious enough to
presume the same intimacy with the gods and goddesses, thereby
drawing attention to the pagan elements of their faiths. What was
a source of strength in these faiths has, thus, become an excuse for
censorship and xenophobia.

One final comment before I end. We are probably entering a
period when the decisive battle will not be between fundamentalism and secularism or between identity politics and normal,

interest-based politics. The battle may well be between religion
in its new, packaged, consumer-friendly version as a political
ideological platform and the subversive spiritualities—to steal
Frederique Apffel Marglin's evocative expression—that are breaking out at the peripheries and the underside of our known world.

Terror, Counter-terror, and Self-destruction
Living with Regimes of Narcissism and Despair

That we have dreamed of this event, that everybody without exception has dreamt of it, because everybody must dream of the destruction of any power hegemonic to that degree—this is unacceptable for Western moral conscience. And yet, it is a fact. ...

It is almost they who did it, but we who wanted it. If one does not take that into account, the event loses all symbolic dimensions to become a pure accident, a purely arbitrary act, the murderous fantasy of a few fanatics, who need then to just be suppressed. But we know very well that this is not the way it is. Thus, all those delirious, counter-phobic exorcisms: because evil is there, everywhere as an obscure object of desire. Without this deep complicity, the event would not have had such repercussions.

This goes much further than hatred for the dominant global power from the disinherited and the exploited, those who fell on the wrong

side of the world order. That malignant desire is in the very heart of
those who share (this order's) benefits.

—Jean Baudrillard[1]

Interpretations of the events of 11 September 2001, and the
diverse political and intellectual responses to them, have oscil-
lated between a concern with the wrath of the disinherited and
exploited and the elements of self-destruction built into a hegemonic system. Keeping in mind Baudrillard's warning, I shall
nonetheless focus here on the rage of those who feel they have
been short-changed by the present global system and have no
future within it. This feeling has acquired an ominous edge in
recent times and developed close links with the self-destructiveness inherent in any global system. The rage often does not have
a specific target, though it is always looking for one; and regimes
and movements that latch on to that free-floating rage can go far.
Indeed, once in a while, their targets too have the same need to
search for and find enemies—to reaffirm their raw power and to
recapture the evaporating sense of mission in the managerial ethics of a global system. The two sides then establish a dyadic bond
that binds them in lethal mutual hatred.[2]

ᘒ

A decade after 11 September 2001, it is pretty obvious that
this time there has been a narrowing of cognitive and emotional
range all around. The global culture of common sense has con-
cluded that it is no longer a matter of realpolitik and hard-eyed,
calculative, interest-based use of terror of the kind favoured by the

[1] Jean Baudrillard, 'The Spirit of Terrorism', *Le Monde*, 2 November 2001,
tr. Rachel Bloul.
[2] Vamik D. Volkan, *The Need to Have Enemies and Allies* (New York: Jason
Aronson, 1988).

mainstream culture of international relations and diplomacy—
as, for instance, the repeated attempts the Central Intelligence
Agency (CIA) has made over the last six decades to assassinate
recalcitrant rulers presumed hostile to the United States—but a
terror that defies rationality and abrogates self-interest, a terror
that is deeply and identifiably cultural. Global common sense
also seems to insist, to judge by the responses to 11 September
2001, that there are only two ways of looking at this link between
terror and culture. One way is to emphasize cultural stereotypes
and the way they hamper intercultural and interreligious amity.
This way presumes that the West with its freedoms—political
and sexual—and its lifestyle, identified in popular imagination
with consumerism and individualism, has come to look like a
form of Satanism to many millennial movements, particularly
those flourishing in Islamic cultures. Multiculturalism and
intercultural dialogue are seen as natural, long-term antidotes
to such deadly stereotypes. But, in the short run, the emphasis
shifts to 'firm' international policing.

The other way is to locate the problem in the worldview
and theology of specific cultures. What look like stereotypes,
prejudices, or scapegoating in the first approach are seen as
expressions of the 'natural' political self of some cultures in the
second. At the moment, Islam looks like the prime carrier of a
political self that is inclined to use terror to achieve political ends,
though some other cultures are not far behind. The American
senator who ridiculed those who wore diapers on their heads, did
not have in his mind only the Muslims; nor did the American
motorist who, when caught while trying to run over a woman
clad in sari, declared that he was only doing his patriotic duty
after 11 September 2001.

The first way, because it includes multiculturalism and
intercultural dialogue, is of course seen as a soft option, the

second as harsh. However, in the short run, the first and second options converge and begin to look a more viable, realistic basis for public policy and decisive action. This particular version of political 'realism' is, however, not new. Terror has been an instrument of statecraft, diplomacy, and political advocacy for centuries. To see it as a new entrant in the global marketplace of politics is to shut one's eyes to the human propensity to hitch terror to organized, ideology-led political praxis. Robespierre said—on behalf of all revolutionaries, one presumes—that without terror, virtue was helpless. Terror, he went on to claim, was virtue itself. When it comes to the serious business of international relations, such connections enjoy intrinsic legitimacy in many cultures of public life that today feign shock and dismay when facing terrorism. Despite recent pretensions, in international politics violence does not have to be justified; non-violence has to be. The mainstream global culture of statecraft insists that the true antidote to terror can only be counter-terror.

In this respect, the killers who struck at New York on 11 September 2001 and the regimes that claim absolute moral superiority over them share some common traits. Both believe that when it comes to Satanic others, all terror is justified as long as it is counter-terror or retributive justice. Both believe that they are chosen and, hence, qualified to deliver life and death in the name of righteous causes. And both are posthumous children of the twentieth century—a century that installed the rights to hone technologies of terror and the capacity to inflict unlimited collateral damage at the centre of public life and public policy. Guernica, Hamburg, Dresden, Nanking, Tokyo, Hiroshima, and Nagasaki are all formidable names in the contemporary imagination of permissible political and strategic weapons. So are the attempts to hitch terror to virtue and efficient governance in a wide range of situations—from Jalianwallah Bagh to Lidice, from Sharpeville to My Lai, and from Palestine to Kashmir. The culpable states have sometimes been autocratic, sometimes democratic. Liberal democracy has not often been a good antidote for state terror. Few are now surprised that some of the iconic defenders of democracy, such as Winston Churchill, were as committed to terror as Robespierre was. Not only was Churchill a co-discoverer of the concept of area bombing, as opposed to strategic bombing, he and the armies of the two most powerful democracies in the world did not intercede when supplied with evidence, including aerial photographs, of Nazi death camps.[3] Terror and counter-terror are normal statecraft, only saying so is not.

Hence also the widespread tendency to dismiss all ideas of fighting terror without using counter-terror as romantic drivel. Hence also the tacit admiration for garrison states like Israel in 'softer' states like Sri Lanka and India and the attempts of such admirers to use Israeli 'expertise', forgetting that Israel has been fighting terror with terror for decades without noteworthy success. All that Israel can really take credit for is that, in a classic instance of identifying with its past oppressors, it has succeeded in turning terrorism into a chronic ailment within its own boundaries, in the process brutalizing its own polity and turning many of its citizens into fanatics and racists.

જ

[3] This is, however, a much debated issue. For a reasonably impartial, brief summary, see Matthew Davis, 'Why Didn't the Allies Bomb Auschwitz?' BBC News, 23 January 2005, news.bbc.uk/2/hi/europe/4175045.stm (accessed on 31 August 2015). For a more detailed discussion, see Michael J. Neufeld and Michael Berenbaum, *The Bombing of Auschwitz: Should the Allies Have Attempted It?* (New York: St. Martin's, 2000).

Against this backdrop has entered a new kind of terrorists during the last few years in Sri Lanka, Palestine, India, Pakistan, and now, the United States and Iraq. The suicide bombers have made their presence felt in roughly twenty countries by now. They come prepared to die and, therefore, are automatically immune to the fear of counter-terrorism. They usually view counter-terrorism—and the reactions to it—as useful means of mobilizing and polarizing communities.[4]

This is one form of political activism that the hedonic, self-interest-based culture of the globalized middle class just cannot handle. It looks like an unwanted war declared by the death-defying on the death-denying. The former thrives on a theology of martyrdom, the latter on a psychology of hard, this-worldly individualism and narcissism, which cannot but wonder what kind of a person one is if one does not want to keep any option open for even glimpsing the future one is fighting for or to care about what might happen to one's family, neighbourhood, or community in the backlash? Living in a hedonic, secularized world, unable to fathom why its secular hedonism seems evil to others, the cultural sensitivities of the globalized middle class, never high, has further narrowed in recent times. To the civilized modern citizen, such suicidal activism looks like the negation of civilization, utterly irrational and perhaps even psychotic.

In the nervous, heated discussions that used to take place on the kamikaze sixty years ago, the doomed pilots usually appeared like strange, robotic killers and carriers of collective pathologies, driven by feudal loyalties, unable to distinguish life from death or good from evil. There have been attempts in recent years to

---

[4] This is recognized, though in the language of the mainstream, in Michael S. Doran, 'Somebody Else's Civil War', *Foreign Affairs*, January–February 2002, 81(1), pp. 22–42.

view the self-sacrifice as an 'irrationality' imposed by ruthless, scheming officers of the Japanese army. To that extent, the kamikaze pilots now look less like perpetrators and more like victims. However, while there was ruthlessness and the Japanese army did knowingly push more than 3,000 young men to death, one cannot ignore the atmosphere of desperation and despair that allowed such a scheme to be acceptable to a sizeable section of the Japanese people.

Recent discussions of the suicide bombers of Hamas, Tamil Tigers of Sri Lanka, Al-Qaeda and sundry terrorist groups in Pakistan and Kashmir are linked to similar imageries and fantasies in the mainstream, global awareness. Hence probably the abortive attempts to rename suicide bombings as homicide bombings. The modern world always seems to be at a loss to figure out how to deter someone who is already determined to die. For most of us, such passions have no place in normal life; it can be only grudgingly accommodated in text books of forensic psychiatry as a combination of criminality and insanity. The expression 'homicide bombing', used as a substitute for 'suicide bombing', is an attempt to endorse this reading. The former sounds more decisively evil, stripped of the touch of ambiguous, insane heroism of the latter. Outside the modern world too, few call it self-sacrifice. For unlike the freedom fighters of India and Ireland, who fasted themselves to death during the colonial period as an act of protest and defiance of their rulers, the self-sacrifice of the suicide bombers also involves sacrificing unwilling, innocent others, what we have now learnt to euphemistically call collateral damage.

Yet, the key cultural-psychological feature of today's suicide bombers and suicide squads, despair, is not unknown to the moderns. In some contexts, the idea of despair has become central to our understanding of contemporary subjectivities and we also admit that it has shaped some of the greatest creative endeavours in arts and some of the most ambitious forays in social thought in our times. Van Gogh, Franz Kafka, or Albert Camus cannot be understood without invoking the idea of despair, nor can be Friedrich Nietzsche or Fyodor Dostoevsky. So powerful has been the explanatory power of the idea of despair that recently Harsha Dehejia, an art historian, has tried to introduce the concept in the Indian classical theory of art, by extending Bharata's theory of *rasas* itself. Dehejia feels that without deploying this construct as a part of Indian theories of art, we just cannot explore contemporary Indian art using Indian categories.[5] One suspects that the desperation one sees in the self-destruction of the new breed of terrorists is the obverse of the same sense of despair that underpins so much of contemporary creativity. This despair expresses itself in strange and alien ways because it comes from defeated cultures that have remained mostly invisible and inaudible.[6]

Out of eighteen names mentioned as members of the suicide squad that struck on 11 September 2001, fifteen were identified as Saudis. They came from a prosperous society where dissent was taboo, where political conformity and silence were extracted through state terror. Arguably, by underwriting the Saudi regime, which presided over Islam's holiest sites and had acquired undeserved reputation in some circles as an exemplary Islamic state, the United States had identified itself as the major source of the sense of desperation in the killers. The violence of 11 September,

---

[5] Harsha Dehejia with Prem Shankar Jha and Ranjit Hoskote, *Despair and Modernity: Reflections from Modern Indian Paintings* (Delhi: Motilal Banarsidass, 2000).

[6] One suspects that appearances notwithstanding, some instances of suicide bombing today are primarily a response to American hegemony, directed not so much at the American army, backed by its ready reserve of 3.9 million men and an annual budget of USD 650 billion, but towards the country's near-total control of the global media.

Johan Galtung and Dietrich Fischer argue, presumes 'a very high level of dehumanization of the victims in the minds of aggressors.'[7] That dehumanization did not come in a day, nor can it be explained away as unprovoked. Pervez Hoodbhoy identifies another kind of dehumanization that turns the suicide bombers into drones that are only killing machines—you turn yourself into a weapon for a cause and for a leader who himself never sacrifices his own life or that of his family members though he routinely sends young recruits to death.[8] That total commitment and blind allegiance not merely become passports to instant salvation, but also the meaning of life. While it is tempting to agree with Hoodbhoy, imputing to hundreds of 'crazed demagogues' such immense persuasive powers and ability to seize control of the minds of worshippers also flies in the face of all psychological knowledge.

Thanks to global news media, we are all too aware of the denominational loyalties of the terrorists who attacked the World Trade Centres. They were Wahhabis, given to an aggressively puritanical form of Islamic revivalism. But all Wahhabis do not turn suicide bombers. Who among them do?

A part-answer to that question, we may find out in the coming years, lies not in the ethnic, religious, or class connections of terrorism but in the fear of cultures that forces us to deny the desperation that has begun to crystallize outside the peripheries of our known world as a new bonding between terror and culture. This desperation may not be preceded by theocide, of the kind Nietzsche talks about, but it may be prompted by a feeling that God may not be dead but has surely gone deaf and blind. Situations like that of Palestine is only one part of the story.

[7] Johan Galtung and Dietrich Fischer, 'The United States, the West and the Rest of the World', unpublished ms.
[8] Pervez Hoodbhoy, 'They Only Know How to Kill: Pakistan's Suicide Bombers are Human Drones', *The Times of India*, 12 March 2008, p. 22.

For the present global political economy has begun to reward all cultivated ignorance of how the unprecedented prosperity and technological optimism in many countries have as their underside utter penury, collapse of life support systems brought about by ecological devastations, threats to cosmologies, and nonspecific hopelessness.[9]

Nothing I have come across reveals the nature of this nihilistic, suicidal despair in some parts of the globe better than the following extract from a journalist's story:

> Late last year,... I paid the last of many visits to ... Brigadier Amanullah, known to his friends as Aman. Aman, in his early fifties and now retired, is lithe and gentle-natured and seemed to me slightly depressed.... [A]s the secretary to Benazir Bhutto. ... [He] also keeps in close touch with old colleagues, who include many powerful people in Pakistan. Aman was once the chief of Pakistan's military intelligence in Sind Province, which borders India. ... That put Aman squarely in the middle of things. ...
>
> Aman noticed me looking at the painting and followed my gaze. ... He told me that one day when she was still Prime Minister, an unknown man, an ordinary Pakistani citizen, had come to the gate of Zardari House with the picture ... Aman said that he was immediately transfixed by the painting. ...
>
> We both looked up at the painting in silence. 'A rocket ship heading to the moon?' I asked.
>
> ... 'No,' he said. 'A nuclear warhead heading to India.'
>
> I thought he was making a joke. ... I told Aman that I was disturbed by the ease with which Pakistanis talk of nuclear war with India.
>
> Aman shook his head. 'No,' he said matter-of-factly. 'This should happen. We should use the bomb.'

[9] That is why one of the most thoughtful intellectual responses to 11 September 2001 remains Wendell Berry, 'In the Presence of Fear', *Resurgence*, January–February 2002, (210), pp. 6–8; see also Jonathan Power, 'For the Arrogance of Power America Now Pays a Terrible Price', TFF Press Info. 127, Transnational Foundation, 13 September 2001.

'For what purpose?' He didn't seem to understand my question. 'In retaliation?' I asked.

'Why not?'

'Or first strike?'

'Why not?

I looked for a sign of irony. None was visible. ...

'We should fire at them and take out a few of their cities—Delhi, Bombay, Calcutta,' he said. 'They should fire back and take Karachi and Lahore. Kill off a hundred or two hundred million people. ... and it would all be over. They have acted so badly toward us; they have been so mean. We should teach them a lesson. It would teach all of us a lesson. There is no future here, and we need to start over. So many people think this. Have you been to the villages of Pakistan, the interior? There is nothing but dire poverty and pain. The children have no education; there is nothing to look forward to. Go into the villages, see the poverty. There is no drinking water. Small children without shoes walk miles for a drink of water. I go to the villages and I want to cry. My children have no future. None of the children of Pakistan have a future. We are surrounded by nothing but war and suffering. ...'

... He told me he was willing to see his children be killed. He repeated that they didn't have any future—his children or any other children.

I asked him if he thought he was alone in his thoughts, and Aman made it clear to me that he was not.[10]

∾

Clash of cultures and civilizations become a possibility not because some cultures suffer from specific psychological stigmata but when, for whatever reason, sizeable sections in a society develop a heightened fear of 'strange' cultures living with other moral universes. This is not a prerogative of the backwaters of

[10] Peter Landesman, 'The Agenda: A Modest Proposal From the Brigadier, What One Prominent Pakistani Thinks His Country Should do with its Atomic Weapons', *The Atlantic Monthly*, March 2002.

the civilized world. Even in societies resonating to slogans like multiculturalism, such slogans often become only a means of tolerance of cultures that are compatible with the dominant pattern of global common sense—cultures that can be safely consumed in the form of ethnic food, arts, museumized artefacts, ethnographies, or, as is happening in the case of Buddhism and Hinduism, packaged theories of salvation severed from the ways of life associated with these faiths. That is why the tacit solipsism of Islamic terrorism and its ability to hijack some of Islam's most sacred symbols is matched today by the narcissism of the policy élite in some countries wedded to the idea of their manifest destiny.

The confrontation becomes more serious when, for a large majority of the world, all rights to diverse visions of the future— all utopians thinking and all indigenous visions of a good society—are subverted by the globally dominant knowledge systems and a globally accessible media as instances of maudlin nostalgia, other-worldly delusions or brazen revivalism. The Southern world's future now, by definition, is nothing other than an edited version of contemporary North. What Europe and North America are today, the folklore of the globalized middleclass claims, the rest of the world will become tomorrow. Once the visions of the future are this narrowly defined, the resulting vacuum is sometimes filled by pathological forms of millennialism, the primary concern which is to negate, challenge, or subvert the seemingly unbreakable global consensus on values.[11] Some of these pathological forms are perfectly compatible with the various editions of fundamentalism floating around in the global marketplace of ideas today. In the liminal world of the

[11] See especially the writings of Ziauddin Sardar on this subject. For instance, Sohail Inayatullah and Gail Boxwell (eds), *Islam, Postmodernism and Other Futures: A Ziauddin Sardar Reader* (London: Pluto Press, 2004).

marginalized and the silenced, desperation embraces millennialism at some corner to redefine violence as a necessary means of
exorcizing one's inner ghosts.

ఇం

11 September, Gandhian activist-scholar Rajiv Vora and the
Swarajpeeth initiative have recently reminded us, was the day
satyagraha was born at Johannesburg in 1906.[12] Satyagraha—
militant non-violence, to use psychoanalyst Erik Erikson's translation, and not passive resistance, as the global media tends to
call it—was born in South Africa when it was a proudly authoritarian, racist, police state, not at all like British India, presided
over by a reportedly benign, liberal colonial regime that, votaries
of political realism assure us, ensured the success of Gandhi's
non-violence. Though the principle and the strategy of militant non-violence was worked out by Gandhi, the first person
to proclaim the principle from a public forum at Johannesburg
was Abdul Gani, a Muslim merchant, and their closest associate was Haji Habib, another Muslim.[13] Does this coincidence
of dates and the Islamic connection something to tell us?

[12] Rajiv Vora, '11 September: *Kaun si aur Kiyun*', Unpublished Hindi paper
circulated by Swarajpeeth and Noviolent Peaceforce, New Delhi, 2005; and
Arshad Qureshi, '11 September 1906: *Ek Nazar*', Unpublished paper circulated by Swarajpeeth and Nonviolent Peaceforce, New Delhi, 2005.

[13] Robert Payne, *The Life and Death of Mahatma Gandhi* (London: Bodley
Head, 1969), p. 163. Recent criticisms of Gandhi's religion-tinged language of
politics as an important cause of divisive politics in South Asia, have not considered the possibility that the secular language of politics may have even lesser
cross-religious and cross-cultural reach in some parts of the world. That, however, is another story. Curious readers may like to look up Ashis Nandy, 'The
Twilight on Certitudes: Secularism, Hindu Nationalism and Other Masks of
Deculturation', in *The Romance of the State and the Fate of Dissent in the Tropics*
(New Delhi: Oxford University Press, 2003), pp. 61–82; and Ashis Nandy,

Recently, there has been animated debate on Robert Pape's proposal, based on empirical data, that suicide bombing is primarily a secular, not religious enterprise.[14] Even without contesting Pape's formulation, it is possible that there are at least two other ways of looking at the religious links of suicide terrorism. One way is to compare the despair-driven, suicidal forms of terror with the suicidal defiance and subversion of authorities through fasting to death, as in the cases of some Irish and Indian freedom fighters, to spot the points of contact between two cultures where violence turns outwards and the points where it turns inwards. Such a comparison might reveal the religious meaning of some of the secular acts of suicide terror as easily as the secular meaning of some avowedly religious forms of self-destruction. Perhaps the two most critical criteria in such a comparison will turn out to be the willingness to couple one's self-sacrifice with the willingness to sacrifice non-combatants and the defences deployed to protect one's innocence about the brutalizing effects of terror on one's own community and that of the targets.

The other way is to look at the two types of self-sacrificial intervention as tendencies or traits within every person or community. As an example, I draw attention to the openly religious, militant non-violence of an Islamic community known all over the world today for its alleged weakness for religion-based terror in Afghanistan and Pakistan. Pathans, the major ethnic community in Afghanistan and in so-called lawless North-West Pakistan, are known for their martial valour and were officially declared a martial race by British India in the nineteenth century. They are

---

Shikha Trivedi, Achyut Yagnik, and Shail Mayaram, *Creating a Nationality: The Ramjanmabhumi Movement and Fear of the Self* (New Delhi: Oxford University Press, 1995).

[14] Robert A. Pape, *Dying to Win: The Strategic Logic of Suicide Terrorism* (New York: Random House, 2005).

today the ultimate symbols of mindless violence in the world. For many, there is continuity between the view of the Pathans as a traditionally violence-prone, martial community and view of the Pathan as naturally predisposed towards fundamentalist violence.

Yet, in India at least, till quite recently the Pathans were also a symbol of militant non-violence of the 'truly' courageous and martial. According to Gandhi himself, they were the finest exponents of militant non-violence, directed against the British imperial regime in the 1930s.[15] The Pathans who participated in the Gandhian struggle—at the height of the movement, there were at least 1,00,000 of them who called themselves Khudai Khidmatgars, God's servants—were the products of the same culture that has produced the Taliban and played host to Osama bin Laden and his entourage.

Can this inconsistency be explained away as only an effect of dedicated fundamentalist clerics, the brutalization in the wake of the anti-Soviet struggle in Afghanistan, or the skill and efficiency of the ISI, Pakistan army's notorious intelligence agency? Or does the contradiction exist in human personality and the Pashtun culture itself?[16] The second possibility cannot be dismissed offhand. The behaviour of the ordinary Afghans after the fall of the Taliban regime suggests that the Taliban enjoyed some

[15] An ethnographic monograph that nevertheless captures the other self of the Pathan very competently is Mukulika Banerjee, *The Pathan Unarmed: Opposition and Memory in the North West Frontier* (Oxford: James Currey, 2000). For a hint that this is not merely dead history but a living memory for many, see Ayesha Khan, 'Mid-Way to Dandi, Meet Red Shirts', *Indian Express*, 22 March 2005. See also the moving film by Terry McLuhan, *The Frontier Gandhi* (2008).
[16] See an insightful, sensitive discussion of the way the same cultural resources can be used legitimize and resist terrorism in Bhikhu Parekh, 'Dialogue with the Terrorists', in *Colonialism, Tradition and Reform: An Analysis of Gandhi's Political Discourse* (New Delhi: Sage, 1989), pp. 139–71.

support of the people they ruled. But most Afghans also seemed genuinely happy to get rid of the harsh, puritanical reign of the Taliban.

℘

Who is the real Pathan? The one sympathetic or obedient to the Taliban or the one celebrating the Taliban's fall? The one known for his martial values or the one who in the 1930s turned out to be a death-defying, non-violent resister, facing ruthless baton charges and firing by the colonial police, never retaliating and never flinching? The Khudai Khidmatgars evidently brought to their non-violence the same fervour that the Afghan terrorists are said to have brought to their militancy. Are the Pathans as ruthless with themselves now as they were when resisting the colonial regime?

I shall avoid answering these questions directly and instead venture a tentative, open-ended comment in the end. Most cultures enjoin non-violence or, at least, seek to reduce the area of violence. These efforts often go hand in hand with cultural theories of unavoidable violence. Only a few like Sparta and the Third Reich glorify, prioritize, or celebrate violence more or less unconditionally as the prime mover in human affairs or as the preferred mode of changing the world. In cultures that fall in the first category, violence and non-violence both exist in the same persons as human potentialities. Studying the life experiences that help actualize only one of the two potentialities are the crucial means of entering the mind of the violent and to understand why in a given context only one of the potentialities is actualized.

I have told my story and, like Aesop, appended a moral to it, too. However, an endnote is perhaps in order. A key factor that has in our times contributed to the growth of massive violence can often—though not always—be traced to the part-collapse of communities and the normative systems they sustained. In many cases, the powerful and the rich have welcomed this collapse as pathway to a freer, more individualistic, transparent, predictable world, more congruent with the dominant theories of progress. But flawed norms, one must remember, are norms nonetheless. The social flux and moral anomie that we see around us have condemned large sections of the humankind to live with a vague sense of loss, anxiety, and anger. They live with a sense of abandonment and a feeling that the vocations, cultural life, and ethics are all being slowly invalidated. Many do not clearly perceive the hand of any agency in these changes; they try to bind anxiety and contain anger through consumerism and immersion in the world of total entertainment. That is called normality. But some others do identify an agency, rightly or wrongly. They end up with free-floating rage perpetually looking for targets or embrace ideologies that promise to supply them with readymade targets of violence. Many forms of terror, particularly of non-state actors come from this anomic rage.

Only by engaging with these experiences and the associated suffering is it possible to battle the worldviews or ideologies that organize vague experiences of injustice, abandonment, and uprooting into a work plan for terror. If one is unwilling to negotiate these life experiences or empathize with the pain and the suffering, if one consistently denies their existence and legitimacy and the normal human tendency to configure such experiences into something culturally meaningful, one contributes to and aggravates the sense of desperation and abandonment in millions. At least one well-known Palestinian psychiatrist has claimed that in west Asia 'it is no longer a question of determining who amongst the Palestinian youth are inclined towards suicide bombing. The question is who does not want to be a suicide bomber.'[17] When you de-recognize these experiences or live as if they were only a psychiatrist's concern, you push the desperate and the abandoned towards a small, closed world of like-minded people who constitute a 'pseudo-community' where non-specific rage is perpetually seeking expression in desperate self-destructiveness masquerading as self-transcending martyrdom. The self-transcendence may be questionable, but the desperation is not.

[17] Eyyead Sarraj, quoted in Chandra Muzaffar, 'Suicide Bombing: Is Another Form of Struggle Possible?' *Just Commentary*, June 2002, 2(6), pp. 1–2.

Humiliation

The Politics and Cultural Psychology of the Limits of Human Degradation

Years ago, Giri Deshingkar, distinguished Sinologist and peace researcher, told me a story that may be, for all I know, apocryphal. When diplomatic negotiations took place after the Boxer Rebellion in 1900 between the defeated Chinese regime and the triumphant Western powers, they ended in a humiliating treaty for China. However, the Chinese diplomats looked at it differently. They had sawed off an imperceptible length from the legs of the chairs on which the Western negotiators sat, so that they spoke to the Chinese from a lower height. The Chinese were convinced that *they* had decisively humiliated the Western powers in the negotiations. The Western diplomats, of course, knew nothing about this, and naturally did not feel humiliated at all.

It is possible that while thinking they had triumphed over the imperial powers, the Chinese also knew they had lost. That awareness may have powered their politically impotent, self-congratulatory venture. I am also ignoring the quasi-therapeutic role the humiliation might have played for the Chinese, who were facing traumatizing disgrace and national crisis. The European diplomats may not have been affected, but the very attempt to humiliate them protected Chinese self-esteem. Human nature is a multilayered affair; people respond to or acknowledge events at many levels. I am merely proposing, as a basic assumption of this analysis, that humiliation in human relations can never be a one-way exchange. Unless the humiliated collaborate by feeling humiliated, you cannot humiliate them, however hard you try. No humiliation is complete unless the humiliated oblige their tormentors by validating their desire to humiliate. The Boxer treaty did not fully humiliate the Chinese, and the Chinese did not humiliate the victorious powers either. Those trying to humiliate may get a kick by doing what they do, but unless there is con-sensual validation from the humiliated, humiliation remains one-sided or takes place only in the eyes of a third party.

It follows, counterintuitive though this may sound, that the humiliated, too, have some control over their tormentors. This control is not overt, given that in a game of humiliation the parties involved often have asymmetric power relations. Yet, sensitive ethnographers and littérateurs have frequently come close to acknowledging that, in India's caste system for instance, while the Savarnas apparently control the varna system, the Dalits also have traditionally controlled the Savarnas through their power to pollute by touch or presence and through the Savarnas' constant fear of pollution.[1] This dyadic relationship explains why,

---

[1] There are, of course, subtler fears that plague oppressors in any system of dominance. V. Geetha talks of accusations of witchcraft against Dalit women as another instance of oppression of the Dalits. But this can be read as another

at moments of crisis or conflict involving Dalits, so much venom is released. Conflicts bring to the fore what is tacit in caste relations and creates in the Savarnas a crippling fear of losing control. When Gandhi insisted that anyone joining his ashrams had to first clean toilets, he was not practising, despite appearances, reverse humiliation as a penance. He was striking at the heart of the compact of humiliation that has tied the Untouchable to the 'Touchable'. He was redefining the idea of pollution. In 1973, the Government of Karnataka banned the practice of carrying night soil. If the government had been sensitive to Gandhi's project, it would have made the ban applicable only to Dalits.

Some are uncomfortable with the proposition that successful humiliation needs acknowledgement from the humiliated to the effect that they are being dishonoured. They believe that persons or groups may be so numbed by institutionalized and regular humiliation that their sensitivities are blunted, and so they do not feel humiliated. A third party has the right, they feel, to declare a situation as humiliating. Such an argument apparently has some validity; those who use it usually have in mind the Dalit predicament—what V. Geetha calls 'the dark narcissism of untouchability'. However, appearances notwithstanding, the argument is absurd and anti-democratic. If some victims do not feel humiliated, others have the right to convince them of their situation. But that gives no one the right to declare, on behalf of someone else, that humiliation has taken place, that the victim has become too used to humiliation to sense it, and, therefore, one can act or speak on behalf of the victim. Let us not forget that Hindu nationalists, too, argue on behalf of all Hindus that Muslims have humiliated Hindus for centuries, and that Hindus who do not admit this

---

admission of oppression by the oppressive and their haunting fear of retributive justice. V. Geetha, 'Bereft of Being: The Humiliations of Untouchability', in Gopal Guru (ed.), *Humiliation: Claims and Context* (New Delhi: Oxford University Press, 2009), pp. 95–107.

are benumbed. Even when not invoking the idea of numbing, the assumption of the right to speak on behalf of the humiliated has its hazards. During the Emergency in 1975–7, when civil rights were suspended in India, sycophantic bureaucrats and ruling party functionaries decided, on behalf of Prime Minister Indira Gandhi, that Gulzar's *Aandhi*, a film apparently based on her complicated relationship with her husband, deserved to be banned because it was humiliating to a democratically elected prime minister.

Rajeev Bhargava pushes the argument about numbing further. He declares that a third party has the right to intercede when a person or group being humiliated cannot sense it, for they are already 'socially dead'.[2] This is a cure worse than the disease, though in recent years it has acquired a certain legitimacy, thanks to the intellectual climate created by the growing global concern with victims of trauma in general, and post-traumatic stress disorders in particular. 'Such is the preoccupation with trauma,' says Vanessa Pupavac, 'that over the last decade, trauma victims have displaced famine victims in Western imagination.'[3] These diagnoses of victimization give social analysts the right to 'pathologize' not only individuals but entire communities and declare them socially dead. When a psychiatrist declares a person as having been numbed by years of oppression or as overly sensitive to perceived humiliation due to deep feelings of inferiority, the diagnosis at least does not generally involve a summary trial of an essentialized collectivity.[4] The use of the idea of social death does.

---

[2] Rajeev Bhargava, 'The Moral Significance of Humiliation', paper presented at the conference on Humiliation, Ranikhet, 7–9 September 2002.

[3] Vanessa Pupavac, 'Patholizing Populations and Colonizing Minds: International Psychosocial Programs in Kosovo', *Alternatives*, 2002, Vol. 27, pp. 489–511, esp. p. 489.

[4] Such trials are now no longer rare. Entire populations are sometimes declared politically 'incompetent' because of a history of violence and trauma.

The situation in India is complicated by a number of excellent and suggestive studies that show that sycophancy or ingratiation, one of the key indices of passive acceptance of humiliation, is often deployed as a Machiavellian tactic to control the powerful and to limit their options.[5] This is specially so when the institutional context is bleary or ill-defined, as inter-caste relations have become in recent times, and also in situations of resource scarcity.[6] These studies suggest that those seemingly gulping or inviting humiliation do so, not because they are reconciled to their lot but because they consider it legitimate manipulative behaviour when confronting the powerful; they think it a small price to pay, to neutralize or contain the dominant in a fluid politics of hierarchies and to gain privileged access to power.

Finally, if we grant a third party the right to declare a situation humiliating, independently of the victim's point of view, what happens when an ethnic or religious community claims it does

---

See the suggestive paper by Pupavac, 'Patholizing Populations and Colonizing Minds'; for the larger issues involved, see also Ellen Herman, *The Romance of American Psychology: Political Culture in the Age of Experts* (Berkeley: University of California Press, 1995).

[5] For example, Janak Pandey and R. Rastogi, 'Machiavellianism and Ingratiation', *The Journal of Social Psychology*, 1979, Vol. 108, pp. 221–5; Janak Pandey, 'Ingratiation as Expected and Manipulative Behaviour in Indian Society', *Social Change*, 1980, Vol. 10, pp. 15–17; and 'Ingratiation Tactics in India', *The Journal of Social Psychology*, 1981, Vol. 113, pp. 147–8; R.C. Tripathi, 'Machiavellianism and Social Manipulation', in Janak Pandey, (ed.), *Perspectives on Experimental Social Psychology* (New Delhi: Concept, 1981), pp. 133–87. See also K. Bohra and Janak Pandey, 'Ingratiation Toward Strangers, Friends, and Bosses', *The Journal of Social Psychology*, 1984, Vol. 122, pp. 217–22.

[6] Janak Pandey, 'Effects of Machiavellianism and Degree of Organizational Formalization on Ingratiation', *Psychologia*, 1981, Vol. 24, pp. 41–6; idem, 'Social Influence Processes', in Pandey, *Perspectives on Experimental Social Psychology*, pp. 55–93; and 'Cross-Cultural Perspectives on Ingratiation', in B. Maher and W. Maher (eds), *Progress in Experimental Personality Research* (New York: Academic Press, 1986), pp. 205–29.

not mean to humiliate anyone by following age-old practices or conventions? Do we accept the claim at face value, or grant others the right to proclaim the community dishonest or hypocritical? Conversely, when some groups claim to have been humiliated, do others have the right to deny those claims? Such questions are becoming important because globalization today is bringing communities into more regular and close contact. The scope for unintended humiliation is growing. The dog-loving English have to now deal with the dog-eating Koreans. The pork-loving Germans and Chinese cannot avoid the pork-shunning Muslims and Jews. The chances of humiliating someone unintentionally have increased enormously.

൏

However, if we accept humiliation as one side of a reciprocal relationship, humiliation can be an interpreter's nightmare. Who humiliates whom, when, and how? Does humiliation have anything to do with changing times and moral standards? When one brings up the subject of colonialism, does one demean only the former colonized societies or also the former colonizing societies? Is a record of victimization more shameful to victims or to those who victimize? Can we assume that colonialism truly ends when both colonizers and the colonized acquire the psychological capacity to see colonialism as a more embarrassing or humiliating memory for the former colonizers?

Thus, I confess that I have always felt uncomfortable with American blacks changing the name of their community according to their changing ideas of what is humiliating and what is not. They were first negroes, and many of them did not like the name because it was associated with slavery and, later, racial discrimination. They became blacks and, after a while, some of them did not like that either, because it ironed away ethnic distinctions. Since then, they have become African Americans. This kind of response declares the locus of control to be outside oneself; the response is a reaction to what others think, and an attempt to revise one's self-definition accordingly.

Yes, the term 'negro' was associated with slavery, and with the term of contempt 'nigger'. But negro also means black and it is still associated with the self-definition of Francophone Africans, who have no option but to use the term because it is the only one available to them in French. 'Noire' just does not have the same ring as black. More importantly, the term 'negro' has been associated with much resistance, protest against oppression, and creativity against immense odds. It is associated with Leopold Senghor's idea of negritude, Paul Robeson's negro spirituals; with W.E.B. Dubois' work on the African cultural heritage of the negroes, their cultures of survival and protest under slavery and after, when slavery ended but discrimination and humiliation did not. 'Black' does not carry these associations. The term African American is, in some ways, worse. It blurs the entire recent past of violence, torture, and exploitation through which Black Americans have passed and links them to their African heritage, about which they know little.

What I dislike most is the tacit admission in such renaming that the memories of slavery and racism are more shameful for blacks than for whites. It is as if blacks had to more carefully and diligently erase their past than those who practised slavery. The whites have not changed their name or ethnic tag, though they carry the heavier historical baggage of slavery. No white has resented being called a white even though that name has been associated with oppression, exploitation, and genocide in most parts of the world and can be used as a term of abuse. I cannot but suspect that the attempt of American blacks to rename themselves is partly based on the belief that it is more honourable to be a master than a slave. I like to believe that, in a future society, after the collapse of racism, calling oneself a negro may be considered an attempt to insult the whites by recalling the days of slavery. Symbols of defiance do sometimes enshrine entire worldviews.

∽

This brings me to my second proposition. While civilization as a process means the gradual abolition or dilution of master–slave relationships, it also means a growing awareness that it is more honourable to be a slave than a master, if not as a viable social or personal choice, at least as a normative and cognitive frame. (To secure wider acceptability for this proposition, I am willing to rephrase it to claim that it is less dishonourable to be a slave than a master.) This is a position different from the one that asserts that it is as dishonourable to be a master as to be a slave. The first presumption—that the slave is morally and cognitively superior—allows a collectivity to 'work through' its past, as psychoanalysts describe the process, and opens up the possibility of wide-ranging creative use of the past. The latter—in practice a façade for the entrenched belief in the master's moral infirmity but cognitive superiority—often prefaces reactive ethnonationalism, built on defences such as projection, displacement, and identification with the aggressor. Above all, it leads to a constant effort to beat the master at his own game.[7]

[7] The ways in which the memories of British colonialism in South and Southeast Asia are deployed constitute an example. As a general rule, countries, regions, and communities that are more self-confident and less plagued by memories of real or imagined humiliation, like persons with robust ego strength, need fewer symbolic reparation and ritual and/or compulsive 'undoing'

I have discussed this issue elsewhere in some detail.[8] Let me confine myself here to its implications for communities trying to escape humiliation and protect their dignity.

ɔ

Humiliation in South Asia is usually a story of separation and the pain of separation. But like the post-Boxer treaty negotiations in China, that story too has a built-in Roshomon effect.

Caste and religion are seen as the main sources of separation in our part of the world. Most people hope that both will dissolve obligingly in an egalitarian modern society, giving way to separations based on non-ascriptive, secular, social divisions that are, for some reason, presumed to be less painful and squalid. Yet, paradoxically, most serious battles waged against caste and reli-

---

of the past. Even their nationalism reflects the lighter burden of the memories they carry. There *is* a difference between a nationalism built on an underlying strain of anti-imperialism which sees itself as heir to an anti-colonial movement and a nationalism that seeks constant national and cultural security by bending or distorting the entire machinery of state and the entire culture of politics to equal the former colonial powers in statecraft and diplomacy. Gandhi, officially remembered in India mainly as a nationalist leader, was sensitive to this issue. Nationalism, to be genuinely anti-imperialist, had to be non-violent, he openly claimed, for armed nationalism was the other name of imperialism. M.K. Gandhi, *The Collected Works of Mahatma Gandhi* (New Delhi: Publications Division, Government of India, 1967), Vol. 25, p. 369. What remained unsaid was that non-violence was the natural political stance of the psychologically healthy, not of political eccentrics and the politically weak who had a poor grasp of the reality around them. To opt for violence as the 'proven' technology of the master is to admit defeat even when the master has been formally defeated.

[8] Ashis Nandy, *The Illegitimacy of Nationalism: Rabindranath Tagore and the Politics of Self* (New Delhi: Oxford University Press, 1994); and idem, *The Intimate Enemy: Loss and Recovery of Self Under Colonialism* (New Delhi: Oxford University Press, 1983).

gious bigotry have used caste and religion, and not secular social categories like class. These battles have weakened caste and religious bigotry socially, but also strengthened them as principles of political mobilization.[9] The dramatic rise of the numerically preponderant lower castes in Indian public life has come through caste mobilization, with its attendant problems. It is only our self-serving, cultivated blindness that stops us from acknowledging that the same may be the case with religion, that we may have to cope with problems associated with religion by deploying religion itself—as an input into the culture of politics and as a principle of political mobilization. Even a hardboiled, modern secularist like B.R. Ambedkar, in order to fight religion-based discrimination and exclusion, had to make a statement by converting to Buddhism, a religion neither immune to exclusion and chauvinism nor to caste-based discrimination (as the Sri Lankan experience shows). In our times, the Dalai Lama and Desmond Tutu have shown how this can be done.

We like to believe that all principles of separation humiliate. They may not. As an old, poor, Muslim riot victim living in Delhi's Jama Masjid area said some years ago in a television interview, 'Previously we did not eat together, but our hearts met. Now we eat together but our hearts do not meet.' Nearness may not merely sour but also implode. Let me go back to a story brought to my notice by Dipesh Chakrabarty, which I consider in many ways paradigmatic.[10] Unfortunately, the story is not widely known; to use it, I shall have to tell it again.

[9] In the case of caste, D.L. Sheth has attempted an insightful stock-taking that explores the long-term political consequences of the process. See D.L. Sheth, 'Secularisation of Caste and Making of New Middle Class', *Economic and Political Weekly*, 21–28 August 1999, 34(5), pp. 2502–10.
[10] Dipesh Chakrabarty, 'Remembered Village: Representation of Hindu-Bengali Memories in the Aftermath of Partition', *Economic and Political Weekly*,

Jasimuddin was the best-known folk poet of Bengal of the twentieth century who was also a devout supporter of the Muslim League and the idea of a separate homeland for the Muslims. He came from a humble background and was a fellow student of the famous radical film director Mrinal Sen in a school at Faridpur (now in Bangladesh). Mrinal's father spotted Jasimuddin's brilliance early and the young Jasimuddin began to visit the Sens, soon becoming virtually a member of the family. An indicator of the intimacy between the budding poet and the Sens was that Jasimuddin used to call Mrinal's mother 'Ma' and the Sens in turn called him by his pet name, Sadhu (literally, 'world renouncer'). As communal politics began to warm up in the 1940s, Jasimuddin and Mrinal's father often had fierce debates, his father supporting conventional nationalism, Jasimuddin its ethnonationalist version.

One day, during the course of such a debate, Jasimuddin asked why the Sens, if they considered him a member of their family, made him eat separately when he dined at their house. This embarrassed everyone, for it was true. Mrinal's mother, with tears in her eyes, explained that it was the servants who objected to Jasimuddin eating with the rest of the family. Indeed, the servants resisted washing the plates he used; she had been washing Jasimuddin's plate herself.

We have no clear picture of how the dialogue ended, nor of the fate of the relationship after the event. However, we can make a few guesses. First, the Hindu servants, themselves of uncertain social status in the family, tried to protect their self-esteem by separating and humiliating Jasimuddin. They must have felt threatened by the closeness of a Muslim to the domestic power

---

10 August 1996, pp. 2143–61. I have discussed this story earlier, for different purposes, in Chapter 3, 'Telling the Story of Communal Conflicts in South Asia: Interim Report on a Search for Defining Myths'.

structure and insisted on their right, as Hindus, to observe the principles of purity and pollution, to reaffirm a social hierarchy that was getting dangerously fuzzy. They were making a point by humiliating the new member of their employer's household who dared to call the mistress of the house 'Ma'—not the way servants in a Bengali household call their women employers so, but the way a surrogate son does. Indeed, one suspects that they were protecting themselves from humiliation by humiliating the new-found 'son' of the family and reducing him to his 'true' stature—a poor Muslim patronized by the family.

The result was that Mrinal's mother's moving gesture—an upper-caste woman washing the plate of her son's Muslim friend, and humiliating herself vis-à-vis her servants to protect her adopted son from humiliation—did not get its due either from an angry young partisan of ethnonationalism or from her own modern son. Jasimuddin *did* feel humiliated, and even the self-abnegation of Mrinal's mother could not erase the hurt beyond a point. However, it is also clear from the story that Jasimuddin felt humiliated at least partly because he had come close and entered the circle of commensality and kinship, and was expecting a different kind of behaviour from the family. It was not distance but nearness that created the problem in the first place.

Do separations, encrypted in principles of commensal taboos, automatically lead to humiliation, as Jasimuddin seemed to believe? Had he not felt humiliated, would it have been because he was numbed to the demands of ritual hierarchy in the closed circles of 'Touchables'? A part-answer lies in an interview Saba Khattak carried out in Pakistan with a woman victim of Partition for a collaborative project on mass violence.[11] The victim firmly

[11] Saba Khattak, unpublished, untitled paper presented at the workshop of the project, 'Reconstructing Lives', Centre for the Study of Developing Societies, Delhi, 2001.

denied that the observation of rules of purity, impurity, pollution, and touch had anything to do with Hindu–Muslim tensions or the violence of Partition. Hindus did not eat with most Hindus in any case, she said. In another variation on the theme, Prafulla Sen, a refugee from the former East Pakistan, though he himself did not believe in caste-based checks on commensality, remembered with great fondness his Muslim friend Sirajuddin Ahmed's father, who was once furious with his son for hosting Prafulla and helping break Prafulla's commensal taboos. The relationship between the two families had spanned two generations; Prafulla's late father too had been a friend of Sirajuddin's father. The latter, on hearing of the transgression, lamented: 'How will I show my face to your father after I die? How shall I tell him that my son helped your son to lose his religion?'[12]

One sees in these episodes three faces of humiliation in a political culture. In the last case, both sides accept separation in some areas of social life as almost a cultural eccentricity, the odd but unavoidable religious practice of a community. The distance that so humiliated Jasimuddin does not poison social relations in the other two cases. One is tempted to add that, if one is not committed to a melting pot model and is ready to view public culture partly as an interplay of contending, incompatible cultures of communities that observe inbuilt limits on interaction, one has to be prepared to confront situations where some degree of tolerance will have to be exercised for rituals and practices that look hierarchical or humiliating from within a melting pot model. I remember my late friend Jaidev Sethi, an activist–scholar and Gandhian, telling me that he had to virtually starve when visiting his ancestral village in Pakistan after a gap of fifty years. No longer having Hindu neighbours, the villagers went by their memories

[12] Anindita Mukhopadhyay, interview with Prafulla Sen, Delhi, 1997.

and reduced Sethi, who did not know how to cook, virtually to tears by affectionately gifting him a huge mass of uncooked green vegetables and cereals. They expected the returning son of the village to observe caste taboos and cook his own food. They did not believe him when he said he ate everything and was perfectly willing to eat at anyone's place.

Such tolerance presumes, however, two relatively autonomous, self-confident communities or persons, something that cannot be said in the case of Dalits. Saba Khattak's case strengthens the argument. In it, familiarity with other cultures assures the respondent that separation is not targeting the respondent or her community specifically. Separation becomes acceptable because two generic, already internally fragmented entities called 'Hindus' and 'Muslims' have emerged and one is able to say, as Khattak's respondent said, that 'they' treat their own kind the way they treat 'us'. In Jasimuddin's case, the closeness of the budding poet to the future film director's family gives separation a different meaning. The threshold of tolerance has been lowered because the two parties have redefined their communities. Both sides are modernized to the extent that they cannot have asymmetrical relationships with each other and hierarchy-tinged separation becomes a marker of humiliation.

I am emboldened to add that Jasimuddin's story is paradigmatic also in the sense that most modern social scientists can empathize with Jasimuddin and Mrinal Sen's point of view, not with the predicament of Jasimuddin's adopted mother or that of her servants. The 'strange', politically incorrect categories of those at the receiving end of a social order are an embarrassment and must be quickly forgotten, presumably for the benefit of the victims themselves. It is a bit like the consistent forgetfulness I have found in the plethora of reports and studies that came out after the massacre of Sikhs in Delhi in 1984. None mentions a recurrent theme in the testimonies of Sikh victims when talking of the complicity of the Indian National Congress and the Rajiv Gandhi regime in the pogrom—'they got us beaten up and killed by the Bhangis (Untouchables).' Some kinds of humiliation, we implicitly recognize, no respectable victim should complain of.

Insensitivity to such situations is what makes the psychological measures of social distance so vacuous in a country like India. Scores of studies were done at one time on intercaste and interreligious relations here with such measures, particularly the Bogardus Social Distance Scale. All of them assumed a graded relationship between different kinds of social interaction. (For instance, if I accept my daughter's marriage to your son, I am closer to you than if I am willing only to dine with you.) In a complex, pluricultural, traditional society, such simple linear relationships do not obtain. Emory Bogardus would have been surprised to hear that in many South Asian communities, despite intermarriage, commensality may not always be possible. An obvious example is of a parent who does not eat at his or her married daughter's place, because custom demands restraint. Intermarriage itself makes some kinds of commensality impossible. (Even in a modern setting, there is George Bernard Shaw's crypto-Biblical injunction, 'Do not do unto others what you would that they do unto you. Their tastes may be different.' I have heard of at least one French family which is happy that their progeny has married into an Indian family but has resisted eating at the home of their in-laws, lest they have to eat Indian food.)

This flux in the meaning of humiliation is well exemplified by one of the darkest periods in South Asia. Pollution and purity acquired entirely different meanings during the Partition riots when, by most conservative estimates, 1,00,000 women were abducted. Strangely, a very large proportion of the abductors married their victims in Punjab. All these abductors could have raped and killed their victims (as some of them did). Why did they marry their victims? How did communities and the families of abductors accept women from enemy communities in a caste society? Unlike Bengal, in Punjab abduction was a three-way traffic. All three religious groups—Hindus, Muslims, and Sikhs—participated in the game, and in all three cases a large number of families, clans, and communities accepted the abducted women. Some of us have even identified villages and urban ghettos where a majority of the elderly women, even today, are women abducted during Partition. Presumably, these women live with their traumata and memories of humiliation. Yet they live with them not as aliens or strangers, but as insiders. How have concepts of pollution and purity worked in these cases? One possibility is that, after humiliating their enemies by stealing their women, the abductors felt morally obliged to protect a semblance of the dignity of their victims by marrying them. Another is that marriage could establish 'honourable victory' or seal the social superiority or equality of the abductors. The concept of a *rakshasa*, or demonic, marriage in India's epic traditions might have supplied a framework of justification for such feelings. Perhaps, for some abductors, the humiliation of the enemy was not complete if they had only raped and abandoned their victims or remained anonymous rapists and killers. Losing one's own woman or capturing others' women took place within a common frame of humiliation and counter-humiliation, defeat and victory. But these are guesses; we do not really know.

Compare this experience with rapes during the 2002 riots in Gujarat where, in many cases, after raping a woman, the rapists set her on fire. Some of the killers justified this by saying they were advised to prevent the multiplication of Muslims through unwanted pregnancies; others said they were told not to leave behind witnesses. The game in Gujarat was not humiliation, but annihilation. In Bosnian genocide, too, rape was used as a well-organized technique of dishonouring and polluting the other, and as a means of systematic deracination. As part of a jury in the Women's Court Against Racism, set up in Durban in 2001, I heard testimonies on the chronic culture of rape under slavery in the United States.[13] One testimony based on the diaries, auto-biographical records, notes, and letters of plantation slaves in the United States claimed that many women knew their mothers and grandmothers had been raped; they were raped themselves; and they could see that their daughters would be raped too. Rape was a part of normal life. It included a component of amoral, nihilistic, destructive humiliation that was anti-life. In the same category fall the cases of two Dalits at Thinniyam, Tiruchi, forced by those belonging to the non-Brahminic, upwardly-mobile Thevar community, to eat human excreta in Tamil Nadu; and the Dalit domestic help who underwent the same treatment in Eastern Nepal at the hands of a Chhetri couple.

Finally, to be aware of the instrumental use of the rhetoric of humiliation, one must also be aware of voluntary or invited humiliation as a technique of political mobilization and consolidation. Humiliation can be imagined and cultivated in response to contemporary political and social needs. First, a record of humiliation can become a badge certifying one's identity and membership of an in-group. Violent nationalism has always carefully nurtured feelings of humiliation, Nazism being its best-known example. However, there are less diabolic versions of cultivated humiliation used as the means of political and social mobility. Some Cochini Jewish immigrants in Israel talk about centuries of oppression in Kerala, whereas their own community

[13] World Court of Women, *Singing in the Dark Times* (Bangalore: Asian Women's Human Rights Council, and Tunis: El Taller, 2002).

in Cochin talk of 2,000 years of non-discrimination and a life
of dignity. Indeed, the Cochin Jews are surprised and amused by
the history of oppression that some Israeli Jews of Indian origin
have concocted.[14] But, in Israeli public culture, there is a rat race
among communities flaunting their experience of oppression and
humiliation; not having a record of ill-treatment is a misfortune in
that society. In that rat race, European Jews have the edge because
their persecution, over the centuries, is one of the key images
around which the self-definition of the Israeli nation-state is built.

When the creation of a feeling of humiliation is part of a political programme, it is not always equally necessary to possess a genuine record of oppression and violence. Ethnonationalists know
this. Hindu nationalism, for instance, talks of many instances of
humiliation that look contrived and fictitious, or as projections
into the past of more recent feelings of inferiority vis-à-vis Islam
and Christianity. Empirical evidence to the effect that no generic
category called Hindus faced these humiliating instances in premodern times—because the vast majority of Hindus did not even
define themselves as Hindus till the nineteenth century—fails to
cut much ice with Hindu nationalists. The sense of humiliation
and feelings of inferiority they have lived with in recent times are
real, history serves as a screen on which to project their perceived
humiliation, and political propaganda works.

ಲ

I have already mentioned the growing use of the technique of
pathologization. That technique is quickly becoming a postcolonial version of the colonial technique of infantilization. It is

[14] Ashis Nandy, 'Time Travel to a Possible Self: Searching for the Alternative
Cosmopolitanism of Cochin', *Time Warps: The Insistent Politics of Silent and
Evasive Pasts* (New Delhi: Permanent Black, 2002), pp. 157–209.

therefore important to remember that though the pathologies of humiliation attract public notice because of their incendiary potential, humiliation can also open up new, creative possibilities. If the capacity to feel humiliated presumes minimum self-esteem, the capacity to withstand or stand up to humiliation, too, presumes ego strength, a sense of mastery over oneself and one's environment. An incapacitating or crippling fear of humiliation may also indicate low self-esteem. This is the other side of Geetha's formulation that humiliation is fundamentally an experience which questions and recasts one's relationship with oneself.[15]

There are many instances when attempts to diminish or narrow the target's self have ended up expanding it. When a racist, white conductor threw Gandhi out of a train compartment in Pietermaritzburg in South Africa, despite Gandhi holding a first class ticket, the conductor did not know that he was gifting the world a new political weapon for the oppressed—militant non-violence. That humiliating encounter in a lonely South African railway station turned out to be a boon not only to the world but also to Gandhi himself. It woke him, as it were, from a stupor. Some forms of humiliation—such as the crawling order enforced in Punjab in the wake of the Jalianwallah Bagh massacre in 1919—degrade and silence the victims, but may also help consolidate new political formations. Others directly create new openings. These consequences have as much to do with the nature of the humiliation as with the nature of the victim.

The experience of Pietermaritzburg may have also sensitized Gandhi to the pedagogic possibilities of milder forms of humiliation. During India's freedom struggle, many found Gandhi's dress disgraceful and his negotiations with the viceroy on an equal footing humiliating. Winston Churchill felt offended by the

[15] Geetha, 'Bereft of Being'.

antics of 'the half-naked faqir'. Others found it provocative and humiliating when, after the famous salt march and the success- ful movement against a newly imposed salt tax, while negotiating with the viceroy, Gandhi took out and sprinkled some illegally made salt on the snacks he was served by the viceregal kitchen. To remove all humiliation from human affairs seems a doubtful possibility. Someone somewhere is always going to feel humili- ated. We probably shall have to console ourselves by acknowledg- ing that sometimes some humiliations can be a means of renewal and re-education for both sides in an unequal partnership.

These creative potentialities exist because humiliation, when it is not an isolated case but a chronic ailment, is usually a politi- cal statement. Some forms of playful counter-humiliation in such circumstances can be a means of defiance. However, to identify such counter-humiliation—often essentially the non-destructive refusal to play assigned roles—one must first acknowledge the contexts in which humiliation becomes chronic. Humiliation breaks out in an epidemic form when the humiliated refuse to abide by well-established institutionalized rules. Humiliation then becomes a means of re-asserting old hierarchies increasingly under stress. That is the crux of the Dalit problem in India today. The humiliation of Dalits does what in other situations is sought to be done through mass murder.

Humiliation becomes a substitute for genocide partly because, unlike the American Indian, a good Dalit has never been a dead Dalit. Though outcastes, Dalits remain within the caste system by being a collection of service castes. If they do not supply these services, others have to perform them, or one would have to opt for self-service. In either case, the result is a quick loss of social status. Humiliating Dalits is a means of avoiding that status loss and the resulting humiliation. This leads to strange anomalies. While studying the Partition violence of 1946–8, we found out

how the Karachi élite and Pakistan's political leadership had to
cajole the Hindu Dalits of Karachi to stay on in the city when
ethnic cleansing was taking place all over northern India. In fact,
when, after the destruction of the Babri mosque in 1992, some
people targeted the Karachi Dalits, they struck work and reduced
the city to a stinking slum. In no time, they were provided armed
security. In a caste society, fears of pollution can supersede
fanaticism.[16]

ɔ

In the classical Hegelian master–slave relationship, one can build
upon Octave Manoni and affirm that the slave, to survive, cannot
but be sensitive to the moods, foibles, and personality dynamics
of the master. The master, on the other hand, can to an extent
afford to objectify his possession; he does not have to internalize
the slave. This splits the slave into two. One part of his or
her personality wants to equal the master, to do to the master
and to others what has been done to him as a slave. Gandhi, in
Hind Swaraj, identifies this as the eagerness to acquire the tiger's
nature, without the tiger.[17] Building upon the original psychoanalytic construct, we can call it identification with a 'remembered'
aggressor, an ego defence that can be seen in full play in today's
Israel and in the cosmology of Hindutva.

In this identification with the aggressor, there is often an
attempt to undo history, real or imaginary, by re-enacting it—with

[16] Unpublished case study presented by Suchitra Subramanyam Sheth at the
Conference on Life History Construction and Mass Violence, organized by
the project on Reconstructing Lives, Centre for the Study of Developing Societies at Udaipur, 25–9 July 2000.
[17] M.K. Gandhi, *Hind Swaraj*, in *Collected Works of Mahatma Gandhi*
(New Delhi: Publications Division, Government of India, 1963), Vol. 4,
pp. 81–208.

oneself on the winning side. This is accompanied by a search for scapegoats, by humiliating whom one can undo the past. Yet, even when such re-enacting and scapegoating succeed, one cannot forget or overcome the past and move on, because one has in the meanwhile redefined oneself and given a central place in one's self to the repeated attempts to reinvoke and undo the past through violence; these attempts have become the means of holding together one's self-definition. Even successful genocidal revenge, directed against real or imaginary enemies, cannot square the balance. For without the triad of scapegoating, undoing, and acting out, such a self-definition faces collapse.

Valentine Daniel describes how, while combating the aggressive evangelism of Christian missionaries, all other religions have in the last hundred years internalized some key categories and features of European Christianity, including the European meaning of religion, turning the twentieth century into a cultural triumph of Western Christianity.[18] To fight humiliation and acquire respectability, according to European concepts of respectability, every major religion in the South has sought to retool itself to conform to a standardized definition of religion.

Daniel's formulation prompts one to question the idea of respectability itself, because, in this instance, respectability means respect from within the Hegelian master's world itself. Such respectability inextricably traps the victims of humiliation in the 'tiger's nature', creating, in the long run, new targets of humiliation. Perhaps the true counterpoint to humiliation is not respect, unless we mean by it self-respect of the kind that goes with what psychologists call ego strength, that too of an order that can survive experiences of humiliation. Perhaps the

[18] Valentine Daniel, 'The Arrogation of Being by the Blind-Spot of Religion', *Hitotsubashi Journal of Social Studies*, July 2001, 33(1), pp. 83–102.

counterpoint to humiliation is empathy. As it happens, empathy is neither a political category nor can it be inculcated through institutional means. In everyday politics, however, it is probably safer to presume that the 'normal' counterpoint to humiliation is the absence of humiliation. This is particularly true of societies where communities are not dead and people expect, from fellow citizens belonging to other communities, not brotherly love but some degree of distant tolerance.[19]

This emphasis on the idea of self-respect is not incidental. In India at least, when one talks of humiliation, one invariably has in mind the Dalits. And when the Dalits talk of humiliation, there is always the presence of a derecognized psychological reality: hostility towards one's own culture and vocation inculcated in the Dalits over generations. Hence, no rhetoric of recovery of indigenous cultures or protection of artisan skills goes far among them. The Dalit commitment to modernity may sometimes be fuzzy and uninformed, but it is usually total. Modernist social reformers have endorsed this self-image by constantly describing the Dalits along only two dimensions: they are poor and they are oppressed; as if the Dalit communities did not have their gods, caste *puranas*, legends, cuisines, and systems of knowledge; as if empowering their culture was to disempower the Dalits. It was against this flattening of the image of the Dalit that the likes of D.R. Nagaraj protested.[20]

To return to our core metaphor, there is the other part of the slave's personality that fights the master by refusing to internalize him, even while acknowledging the master's humanity. It is as if the slave recognized, as a key to survival, that in the long

[19] Nandy, 'Time Travel to a Possible Self'.
[20] For instance, D.R. Nagaraj, 'From Political Rage to Cultural Affirmation: Notes on the Kannada Dalit Poet-Activist Siddalingaiah', *India International Quarterly*, Winter 1994, 21(4), pp. 15–26.

run it was better to be a slave than a master. That is the ultimate meaning of rebellion and the guarantee of the destruction of the master–slave relationship, not glib talk of equality and justice.

Thus, we come back to square one and to the proposition that the growth of civilization itself is defined by growth of the awareness that the slave enjoys not merely moral but also cognitive superiority over the master. The master has more reasons to refashion his identity than the slave has. This is what I meant when I confessed my discomfort with African Americans changing their name because of the history of slavery, while their white compatriots strut around as whites.

However, I should not end this essay without taking note of a basic contradiction in the master's personality. It arises from the basic incompatibility between humiliation and what Aimé Césaire calls, 'thingification'.[21] Institutionalized slavery requires thingification. One has to objectify a human being to efficiently use him or her like a machine or a domesticated animal; one has to redefine the slave as only a factor in production. But then, one cannot humiliate things or animals because, as I have argued already, the victims must grasp their humiliation for humiliation to succeed. Humiliation is a human situation; it can never be extra- or trans-human. To humiliate someone, you have to grant your target human sensitivity. To that extent, you also have to be willing to be a captive to the will of the humiliated. In this respect, humiliation is a bit like torture. One is a successful torturer only when one's victim begs for forgiveness and screams for mercy to satisfy the torturer's sense of power, control, or sadism and thus endorse the torturer's sense of mastery over himself. But think of the torturer whose victims laugh at him and deny his ability to

---

[21] Aimé Césaire, *Discourse on Colonialism*, tr. Joan Pinkham (New York and London: Monthly Review Press, 1972).

inflict pain and, thus, gradually reduce the torturer to a frustrated, desperate, and even humiliated being, struggling to maintain his dignity.[22]

Humiliation can destroy people only by bringing them closer and inducing them to share categories and establish common criteria. Humiliation cannot survive without some degree of consensual validation. Humiliation dissolves when the dyadic bonding—and the culture that scaffolds it—is disowned by at least one of the two sides.

---

[22] In Romain Gary's novel, *The Dance of Genghis Cohn* (Harmondsworth: Penguin, 1978), the anti-hero, former SS officer Schatz, is possessed by the ghost of Genghis Cohn, a Jewish comedian, who became Schatz's victim when an inmate of Auschwitz. Cohn remains, even in death, defiant and insolent. He haunts Schatz by displaying his only apparently impotent, comic defiance.

M oktern oldernity and the
Sense of Loss

Or Why Bhansali's *Devdas* Defied
Experts to Become a Box Office Hit

In the lives of emperors there is a moment which follows pride in the
boundless extension of the territories we have conquered, and the mel-
ancholy and relief of knowing we shall soon give up any thought of
knowing and understanding them. There is a sense of emptiness that
comes over us at evening, ... It is the desperate moment when we discover that this empire, which had seemed to us the sum of all wonders,
is an endless, formless ruin, that corruption's gangrene has spread too far
to be healed by our sceptre, that the triumph over enemy sovereigns has
made us the heirs of their long undoing.

—Italo Calvino, *Invisible Cities*[1]

---

[1] Italo Calvino, *Invisible Cities*, tr. W. Weaver (London: Vintage, 1997), p. 5.

In the political cultures of Asian and African societies, where colonialism helped set up a binary opposition between tradition and modernity, tradition usually has two meanings. The first meaning insists that tradition is what modernity is not and, hence, tends to be hostile to reason and democratic spirit, frozen, rigid, and insensitive to new knowledge. This meaning often goes with vehement pleas to the natives to shed their prejudices and mutual animosities and learn from the country's former rulers and its brand-new, modern élite the beauties of rationality, flexibility, and tolerance. Those who make these pleas with evangelical zeal often behave as plaintiffs, witnesses, jurors, and judges at the same time. This meaning of tradition may not be shared by many social thinkers or researchers, but it remains an important strain in many cultures of politics, all the same.

However, the use of traditions as an antonym of modernity is not always a monopoly of hollow or insensitive authorities or of the ill-educated. Some very distinguished thinkers—from Rammohun Roy to Mohandas Gandhi to Ananda Coomaraswamy—have creatively deployed the same dichotomy, as a variant of Weberian ideal-types, during the last 200 years. Using this negative definition—tradition is what modernity is not—some of the finest minds in Asia and Africa have assessed and critiqued the contemporary, to re-envision, tame, or 'nativize' modernity or breed alternative visions of a good society, informed with but not dominated by the Enlightenment values. These alternatives are not controlled by traditions; the idea of tradition only facilitates a journey into the interiors of self—to search for resources that may allow one to transcend the limits set by our times. In the West, in recent decades, this has been the project of some like Ivan Illich and a section of the ecologists, to give two random examples. In South Asia, this project used to be once epitomized by the worldview of Mohandas Gandhi but has survived in a diffused, scattered form in many activist-scholars ranging from Vandana Shiva to Ziauddin Sardar to Claude Alvares.

There is another meaning of tradition becoming popular in some postcolonial societies and, now, many Muslim societies. 'True' traditions, it is said, are often compatible with modernity and need to be protected against distortions and misuse by the ill-motivated. In modern India, for instance, tradition has come to mean for many the canonical texts of various religions. If you happen to know the Upanishads, the Bible, or the Quran first-hand or have some exposure to Sanskrit or Arabic, you acquire the right to talk incessantly and authoritatively of traditions and proclaim such texts to be perfectly consistent with the values dear to post-seventeenth-century Europe. A new recruit to the cause, Amartya Sen, when he claims that he can read the Sanskrit classics of India first-hand and does not have to leave their interpretation to Hindu chauvinists, is obviously sympathetic to this meaning. 'Low' culture everywhere embarrasses the élite, for it looks riddled with superstitions and crudities and seems a chaotic, unmanageable mass of practices that cannot be easily mobilized to defend national self-esteem in the global middle-class culture. Such practices always seem impervious to the control of a modern nation-state.

Hence, most of those using traditions in the second sense have never seriously examined the traditions of communities even when they are as hoary as the well-known classics—from the healing systems and agricultural practices of some of the ribal communities, such as the Santhals and the Maria Gonds, to the Kerala School of mathematics and the complex, sophisticated musical traditions of numerous castes and tribes of Rajasthan. Though things are changing, most modern Indians, except for professional anthropologists and folklorists, do not think of such lowbrow

stuff when speaking of traditions. When they assess traditions—
to create a space for lofty ideas such as modernity, development,
secularism, or progress in India's political culture—they remain
confined within the familiar universe of the canonical texts. They
want India to be diverse, but only as long as that diversity is house-
broken and does not have the potentiality to subvert modernity.
Their pluralism is a bit like that of a woman student belonging to
India's miniscule Jain community, told a colleague of mine that her
father, being very liberal, would allow her to marry anyone—from
a dark-hued African to a slit-eyed Chinese—as long as he was a
Jain.

As this second approach to tradition seeks to deny ethnic
chauvinists and religious bigots the support of sacred texts, I do
not want to be too harsh on it, however limited or slanted its
idea of tradition. Otherwise, one could have pointed out that
such an instrumental view of traditions can as easily be made
to serve some rather demonic purposes of those busy 'distilling
their frenzy from some academic scribbler of a few years back',
as John Maynard Keynes once described them. To take such an
approach seriously is to be captive to the culture of the Western-
educated, urban, middle classes and their borrowed ideas of
progress, rationality, and future that have come to dominate our
public life. In any case, my concern here is neither Indian traditions nor its detractors. It is to propose that, as an ideology, modernism and the conjoint idea of progress in the Southern world
has rarely been creative, except in the visual arts, some forms of
literature like poetry and in dance and music, that is, in sectors
that are by definition under-socialized and relatively impervious
to the ravages of ideology.

This inability of modernity to release the creative ener-
gies of large sections of people of the region, when it comes to
social knowledge, has many causes. These causes have often

been explored in depth, both by those who have lamented the mimicry and obsequiousness in the social sciences in the South and by those who see a stronger dose of modernity as the patented cure for the ills of modernity. Neither side has seriously explored the reasons for this sterility in the expensively educated, Westernized Asians and Africans who otherwise navigate the modern world with such ease and panache. This failure to explore, too, may not be accidental and there may be an ideologically driven disinclination behind it. It is to that I shall now turn.

cs

Modernity in the Southern world tends to be sterile in social knowledge because it lacks a component associated with many great modern artists, writers, and thinkers elsewhere: a sense of loss brought about by the all-round, decisive victory of modernity itself. In arts, this sense of loss can, unknown to an artist, creep into creative work; in organized thought and social research, it has to be recognized and built into one's theoretical scheme. That in turn is difficult for two reasons. First, the ideology of modernity insists that, while making choices, if the gains outweigh the losses, one must celebrate the gains and forget the losses, in order to move on. To be concerned with the losses is maudlin, self-indulgent nostalgia. Second, there is the widespread fear that to allow the past to criticize the present in the name of traditions is a dangerous pastime that plays into the hands of revivalism and millennialism.

Neither of the positions manage to fully erase traditions. Both only drive traditions underground. Elsewhere, I have described how a gifted filmmaker, Mrinal Sen, aggressively urbane and modern, rejects the very idea of the relevance of his childhood memories of Faridpur in Bangladesh as avoidable nostalgia. Yet, in his most intimate creative moments, he has to return to these memories to grapple with the ghosts from his past and, ultimately, to mourn for the 'home' he has abandoned.[2] And so does film-maker Satyajit Ray, a hard-boiled modernist, in his last film *Agantuk*. Both can get away with this anomaly because they are creative artists, not academics. Few serious modern thinkers in the Afro-Asian world have tried to take the same liberties self-consciously. Among those whose works and lives I know something about, a few like Girindrasekhar Bose, the first non-Western psychoanalyst, who in his more creative moments sought to locate psychoanalysis in Indian traditions and not the other way round, sometimes came close to it. But he did so by default, not design. Social sciences have to seek internal consistency and the way an artist or film-maker can mourn the passage or defeat of the premodern and the non-modern is not probably possible in academic disciplines.[3] Bose's project did include an element of self-consciousness, perhaps because psychoanalysis allowed some space for the past in its theoretical frame. Bose reserved a crucial part of his self for his Bengali writings, as virtually a secret self. For his international audience, he was more conventional, staid and, if I may add, less creative.[4]

[2] Ashis Nandy, *An Ambiguous Journey to the City: The Village and Other Odd Ruins of the Self in the Indian Imagination* (New Delhi: Oxford University Press, 2001), ch. 3.

[3] Ashis Nandy, 'Satyajit Ray's India: Cinema, Creativity and Cultural Nationalism', in Italo Spinelli (ed.), *Indian Summer: Films, Filmmakers and Stars between Ray and Bollywood* (Locarno: Edizioni Olivares, 2002), pp. 24–33.

[4] Ashis Nandy, 'The Savage Freud: The First Non–Western Psychoanalyst and the Politics of Secret Selves in Colonial India', *The Savage Self and Other Essays in Possible and Retrievable Selves* (New Delhi: Oxford University Press, 1995), pp. 81–144.

There is a reason for maintaining such double ledgers. Modernity in much of the Southern world obtains in pockets. These pockets are usually surrounded by the definitive presence of traditions—living, vibrant, and besieged but constantly threatening to rebound. But to the moderns it is modernity that seems besieged and a badge of dissent, despite its growing links with the powerful and the rich. Asian and African intellectuals who are beneficiaries of these links have no incentive to mount a scrutiny that will reveal that they are part of a winning coalition, not part of a threatened minority. They have chosen to live in a narcissistic regime of modernity-as-a-besieged-utopia.

Years ago, I encountered Theodor Adorno's belief that one could be closer to truth when one went against the interests of one's own class. Adorno was not speaking of 'declassing', the patented stratagem that has pushed many radical thinkers and activists to claim for themselves the status of declassed vanguards and to redefine entire communities as dumb victims waiting forever to be emancipated by their intellectual or revolutionary benefactors. I like to imagine that Adorno was anticipating the emergence of a psychotherapeutic state which subtly reduces its disaffected citizenry to second-class status by declaring them incapable of comprehending or articulating the 'truth' about their own suffering.[5] Dissent from the modernist orthodoxy in such a state is punished not as a crime but treated as a form of neurosis or inability to adjust to life.

It is the sensitivity to such issues of dominance, exercised through categories that are bequests of the modern concepts

---

[5] See a more extended discussion of the issue in Ashis Nandy, 'The Twentieth Century: The Ambivalent Homecoming of Homo Psychologicus', *Hitotsubashi Journal of Social Studies*, July 2001, 33(1), pp. 21–33; and 'Humiliation: Politics and Cultural Psychology of the Limits of Human Degradation', *Time Treks: The Future of Old and New Despotisms* (Delhi: Permanent Black, 2007), pp. 1–22.

of expertise and scientific rationality, which have pushed some thinkers to flirt with the idea of loss. Friedrich Nietzsche, who sensed this loss most deeply, made sure that in his version of critical theory, modernity was marked by loss of faith and theocide, and these gave the contemporary human relationships and social institutions a different tonality. Modernity to him was inevitable, but it could not but be tinged by the awareness that the human self was no longer secure in death-transcending faith; it had to learn to live with constant, uncertain negotiations with mortality. Some have found a similar touch of melancholia and pessimism in the works of even Max Weber, seemingly a champion of modern rationality. And there are, of course, William Blake and Karl Polanyi, whose critiques of the urban-industrial civilization can be read as laments for a lost world populated by more plural visions of a desirable society.

Of the two most influential children of the Enlightenment, Karl Marx was not particularly comfortable in admitting any sense of loss, but spoke nonetheless of primitive communism in a way that made it look like a flawed or doomed premodern, pastoral utopia. The loss of that utopia was the price the colonized societies pay to cross the precincts of modernity and to move towards 'adult' communism. Presumably because history, as a synonym of evolutionary progress, forced one to choose bloodthirsty capitalism over primitive communism. In a few second-generation Marxists like Ernst Bloch and, less directly, Joseph Needham, this tacit sense of loss becomes a serious presence, though only in Bloch does it acquire some semblance of theoretical status.

For Sigmund Freud, too, modernity is a stage of civilization where the combined pressures of repression, denial, and rationalization shape the civilization's built-in discontents. What looks like freedom is often purchased at the cost of losing touch with one's instinctual self. Indeed, by repressing crucial parts of one's self, either by isolating them off or by moving away from a life animated by living myths into a narrower range of private fantasies, we precariously eke out our psychological life under the constant threat of a banished self staging an unwelcome return through illnesses of mind. Neuroses are markers of the sacrifices that one has made to prove oneself a loyal devotee of the ideas of progress and civilization. The short-lived attempts by the likes of Herbert Marcuse to give a central place to ideas like polymorphous perverse and the use of the double meaning of repression, too, can be read as parts of the same story.

చ౨

This sharp, painful sense of loss is missing in most Southern social scientists and social thinkers. This is only partly because they still live alongside many powerful, influential, self-confident premodern and non-modern structures that are refusing to dutifully collapse. More importantly, many of these social researchers have opted for modernism as a defiance of their early authorities, within family or outside, and any compromise with pre- or post- or non-modern theoretical frames becomes for them a docile oedipal compact. They cannot permit themselves any self-doubt.

For them modernity, as framed by the Enlightenment vision, is a zealous God. Their commitment to it gives them a sense of belonging to a community, to compensate for the older communities they have disowned or from which they have been prised out. In a society that has not experienced a complete hegemony of the modern, where modernity is still a minority consciousness, the presumed community of the moderns not merely ensures a degree of psychological security, but also underwrites for many social scientists and thinkers their role as vanguards and pace-setters for the rest of the society, ever ready to bear the brown man's burden to improve or brush up the personalities of the underprivileged, and bring them into the modern world that they, the vanguards and the pace-setters, inhabit. Such projects pay handsome dividends, too, in the present global order and there has grown a vested interest in redefining entire communities as the poor and the exploited. As if such communities did not have any identity besides that. As if they were without any culture worth the name and without any knowledge that might give their ideas and categories autonomous cognitive status even in the battle against poverty and exploitation. The triumphalism and zealotry of the idea of progress have become an open assault on the dignity of the underprivileged.

Criticisms of modernity have not been unknown to modernity. In fact, they have been a valued part of modernity. In the post-World War II world—after Auschwitz, Hiroshima, and the Gulags—it is doubtful if modernity is complete without a critique of modernity. But such criticisms are expected to come from the moderns. When they come from outside, they are seen as dangerous or puerile. Traditions are only allowed to establish their compatibility with modernity as part of a rather pathetic plea to be allowed to survive.

Even that compatibility must be established within a set format and clear-cut conventions. For many Southern ideologues of tradition, tradition has come to mean mainly defensive invocation of classical thought and antiquity. The modernity of traditions has become a source of cultural pride, a prop for cultural nationalism. The compatibility between Vedanta and quantum physics, Zen and psychotherapy, are now the subjects of bestsellers. Few dare to reverse the process and justify or criticize nuclear power or stem cell research from within the frame of Islamic ethics or Shaiva Siddhanta. At the same time, any attempt to take seriously living traditions—there is no dearth of them in the South—looks like an obscurantist ploy. Yet, these traditions have learnt to live with internal and external criticisms, more trenchant than what modern sciences or modern political and social thought face. These criticisms come not merely from the moderns, but also from the sheer diversity of traditions and lifestyles. The hundreds of versions of traditions in South Asia, for instance, have been constantly conversing, debating, quarrelling, or criticizing each other. Conversations among religions, sects, and philosophical schools—as also among healing systems, agronomies, and craft traditions—have been going on for centuries outside the ear-shot of those who talk animatedly of dialogue of civilizations. Criticisms also come from the cross-talk of life—from everyday experiences that negate, endorse, ignore, or bypass some tradition or other.

Today, these may not be enough and it may have become imperative to inject a degree of deliberation into the process. I have tried to do so by using the expression 'critical traditionalism' as a necessary component of theoretical frames that seek to reaffirm democratic principles at a time when the global triumph of democracy has come to overlie a deep fear of democracy, primarily a fear of what ordinary citizens, defying experts and specialists, might bring into public life by way of their political and social preferences. I have used the expression mainly to reinstate the dignity and intellectual relevance of everyday life of persons and communities that live with and in traditions, reinvented or otherwise. Actually, such tradtions do not have to be reinvented; they are constantly worked upon by daily life and new experiences. I have even counterposed such traditions against critical modernity, a strand of consciousness that may have limited relevance to the Afro-Asian world but which seems highly relevant to a galaxy of contemporary thinkers who are internal critics or dissenting children of the Enlightenment.[6]

However, these frames often tend to turn overly cognitive to serve the needs of creative social, political, and artistic interventions, when transplanted to the tropics. Hence the need for something not beyond our intellectual control but in better touch with our intuitive, empathetic selves. Here lies the relevance of the sense of loss that has powered the thought of some of those who have made the best use of modernity. Creativity at one plane is a reparative move—a form of expiation or undoing of our inner destructiveness—and this sense of loss yields categories more sensitive to the plight of those who are being gleefully deposited in the sprawling waste yard of History. It humanizes social change.

Exactly as a sense of loss acts as a corrective or a counterpoint to the easy optimism of the currently dominant theories of progress, encoded in nineteenth-century ideologies of a desirable society and good life, there has to be some degree of robust optimism—an engagement with the future that transcends history but shuns millennialism—to power the grassroots theories of critical traditionalism today. This is not the optimism and that comes from a glib acceptance of an apparently inevitable, Leibnitzian, best-of-all-possible worlds. I am speaking of visions carrying the weight of the experience of a 'sense of loss', the way Freud's cosmology carries its burden of a tragic vision of life. After all, in the last 150 years we have seen enormous suffering inflicted on unsuspecting citizens living their normal lives in the name of historical necessities and developmental compulsions.

A concern or engagement with the future can be one way of correcting uncritical traditionalism and deepen one's involvement

---

[6] Ashis Nandy, 'Cultural Frames for Social Transformation: A Credo', *Alternatives*, January 1987, 12(1), pp. 113–23.

with the political status of the traditions of the defeated and the marginalized. Protecting plural visions of desirable societies is a futuristic enterprise. These engagements with the future may be episodic because they have to build upon an oscillation between the past and the future. There is no respite from the future when one grapples with traditions, exactly as one cannot avoid the past when addressing the issue of modernity. That future may be utopian or dystopic, it may be seemingly beyond our control, but as we intervene in the present, we cannot but unwittingly work on new constructions of the past and the future.[7]

This makes the enterprise doubly open-ended because the ideas of culture and tradition used here are already fuzzy and permeable. But then, they are fuzzy and permeable because they have to be kept fuzzy and permeable. If anthropologists and practitioners of cultural studies can live and work with scores of different meanings of the term culture—as most introductory textbooks of anthropology and cultural studies make clear in their first chapters—the few who argue that a celebration of the worldviews of the defeated have something to offer, at least to the defeated and the marginalized, should surely be allowed to function with the blurred edges of the concepts of culture and tradition. In any case, my job here is not to be a ventriloquist's voice for the oppressed, their suffering and resistance. They are quite capable of speaking for themselves. I am trying to reach out to people like me—and to myself—to get a glimpse of the other possible worlds of knowledge open to us. The very search for other such worlds discourages the known world of knowledge to claim sanctity or infallibility in the name of its privileged access to truth and social

[7] See Jim Hick's elegant, succinct treatment of the theme in a review article on Bruno Latour's *We Have Never Been Modern* and Ivan Illich's *In the Vineyard of the Text*. Jim Hick, 'Forward into the Past', *Postmodern Culture*, 1994, 4(3), http://pmc.iath.virginia.edu (accessed on 6 September 2015).

ethics. Even if all the worlds of knowledge for which I have tried
to create political space turn out to be false trails—I hope they are
not—I shall not be heartbroken. The exploration and the play, by
themselves, teach us some tolerance of ambiguities and give us
confidence in our ability to live with porous boundaries of self.
Both are vital ingredients in human creativity and psychological
health, as a series of empirical studies of creativity have shown.[8]

This is not an indirect plea for translation of opaque cultural
strands into familiar dialects, but an attempt to guess why the pursuit of modern social knowledge has been frequently so sterile in
the southern hemisphere, why the occasional spectacular success
of a few have merely underlined the imitative, conformist, repetitious nature of much of the enterprise called social sciences. That
imitativeness cannot be tackled by ensuring the transparency that
modern social knowledge systems seek through ethnographies of
other cultures and alien systems of knowledge. Indeed, that transparency might be fatal for many small communities and cultures,
which survive on the absence of intercultural communication and
on their ability to be obstinately inscrutable. The late literary theorist, D.R. Nagaraj, used to talk of many traditional worldviews,
epistemic systems, forms of praxis, and non-theorized practice
that tended to remain 'playfully incommunicative.' I have written
about that absence of communication; I hope someday to capture something of the playfulness.

∾

In arts and literature, the absence of a sense of loss has not often
cramped creativity because, after a point, the artistic vision

---

[8] For random examples, see Frank Barron, *Creativity and Personal Freedom*
(Princeton, New Jersey: Van Nostrand, 1968); and Rollo May, *The Courage to
Create* (New York: Norton, 1994).

tends to be less socialized and, in the hands of the creative person, never fully driven by theories or ideologies. Indeed, defying the artist and the writer, the sense of loss may intrude into their work, even when they happen to be minor figures or represent popular culture or taste. Let me give a recent example from popular Bombay cinema, which continues to be its usual anti-cinematic self, mixing the carnivalesque with elements of a village fare and allowing the popular to supersede the inner needs of the film-maker.

In circa 2002 was released Sanjay Leela Bhansali's new, sumptuous, Hindi version of the movie *Devdas*, based on Saratchandra Chattopadhyay's popular Bengali novel of the same name. There had been at least twenty film versions of *Devdas* in various Indian languages. In addition, Devdas, the hero of the novel, has periodically made his appearance in various guises throughout the career of popular cinema in India, to the chagrin of distinguished film critics like Chidananda Dasgupta.[9] The novel is the story of a young man devastated by the arranged marriage of his lover, who seeks solace and self-destruction in alcohol and a prostitute who falls in love with him in a city. As the hero nears his end, he makes a doomed attempt to return to his village for one last time.

Though it can read as a simple love story, *Devdas* is also powered by the underlying theme of a person estranged from his village—and angry with its suffocating embrace—trying to return to its uterine warmth after his encounter with a colonial metropolis. *Devdas*, though the work of a famous writer,

---

[9] Chidananda Dasgupta, *The Painted Face: Studies in India's Popular Cinema* (New Delhi: Roli Books, 1991), p. 29: '... It is surprising that this immature piece of fiction should have created such an archetypal hero, a romantic, self-indulgent weakling, who finds solace in drink and the bosom of a golden-hearted prostitute. The character of Devdas has been reincarnated a hundred times in Indian cinema under many guises; its ghost refuses to die.'

is no classic. Nor has it much to say about modernity and its vicissitudes, though there is in it a built-in criticism of traditional caste hierarchy and a soulless city. Its author wrote it as a simple love story when he was less than twenty years old and never thought much of it himself, though he liked its film version directed by Pramathesh Barua.[10]

Bhansali's new *Devdas* was immensely expensive and was not expected to recover its costs. A well-known film director, Kalpana Lajmi, said in a newspaper column that the hero of *Devdas* was a loser and was unlikely to move audiences in contemporary India. The box office proved all the film's critics wrong; the Indian spectator's fascination with *Devdas*, which began when Nitin Bose made the first silent movie version of the novel in 1930s, had still not ended.

Lajmi did not suspect that *Devdas*, underneath its simple story of lost love, is also a story of lost innocence and a lost village. These losses are set against the seductive glitter of urban anonymity, impersonality, and lonely individualism and their false promises in an India where one is not supposed to talk about such losses. *Devdas* succeeds by failing to conform to the established canons of modern aesthetics.

Conventional wisdom now acknowledges that the world of cinema and cricket are psychologically adjacent to each other in India. That adjacency, too, has something to tell us. Traditional cricket, with its mannered, genteel graciousness—some English cricket writers like Neville Cardus do talk of cricket 'our gentle

---

[10] A more detailed analysis of the film and its maker, Pramathesh Chandra Barua, is in Ashis Nandy, 'The City as the Invitation to an Antique Death: Pramathesh Chandra Barua and the Origins of the Terribly Effeminate, Maudlin, Self-Destructive Heroes of Indian Cinema', in *An Ambiguous Journey to the City: The Village and Other Odd Ruins of the Self in the Indian Imagination* (New Delhi: Oxford University Press, 2007), pp. 42–71.

village game' and its 'pre-industrial' values—and its lively nineteenth-century criticism of the algorithm of life in early twenty-
first century. Even the carnivalesque chaos that is common to
popular cinema and cricket in India—and comes packaged in
trite conventionalities—is like a necessary part of a mythogra-
phy of life in which the facile acceptance of Enlightenment values
carries with it subtle subversion of these values themselves. The
audience keeps open the future by accessing a past that may be
already irrevocably lost, but survives as a retrievable dream and
also possibly as a partly accessible, alternative self at the margin
of one's awareness.[11]

જી

Finally, a word on the nature of the political culture of knowledge
through which we see the problem of loss in a world sold to progressivism, where all ideas of loss are predefined as crippling nostalgia. Till now the efforts of ecologists to throw a spanner into
the machine of progress by resacralizing nature and the efforts of
some feminists to demagicalize the idea of production by
resacralizing the idea of reproduction have looked cultish to
many. These efforts may gain new political momentum in the
backwaters of Asia and Africa.

As I have already said, some Western thinkers, artists, and
writers, beginning with Jean-Jacques Rousseau, have relocated
the idea of loss in a revitalized concept of primitivism. The pastoral for others has become an infantile, prerational utopianism
that pluralizes the future. The South has no obligation to get
into this debate or sheepishly accept the current global hierarchy of scholars and authoritative readings of their work. It can

---

[11] Ashis Nandy, *The Tao of Cricket: On Games of Destiny and the Destiny of
Games* (New Delhi: Oxford University Press, 2000).

surely set up its own criteria to reassess Western thought in ways that may look bizarre to the West but are congruent with cultural survival in the South. The South may insist that the so-called romantic is a perfectly valid, *realistic* stratagem to defy conventionality in the hot and humid tropics. The stratagem reverses the social-evolutionary presumptions of the urban-industrial vision; it refuses to see the pastoral as an earlier stage of civilization, now fortunately extinct, and can turn it into a baseline for envisioning new forms of post-industrial life. Likewise, 'cultural nostalgia'—including return to reinvented traditions—may be deployed to read into the Afro-Asian past the potentiality of subverting the linear concept of historicized time, to pluralize the idea of a desirable society and keep open the future for societies that are being forced to view their future as only an edited version of contemporary Europe and North America.

These are probably the reasons why the idea of the pastoral was picked up by a number of non-Western thinkers, Mohandas Karamchand Gandhi being the most conspicuous among them. What looks like a lament for the past in Gandhi can be read as an attempt to conceptualize the future of Southern societies outside the steel-frame of history forged in nineteenth-century Europe. It is no accident that Gandhi was entirely a product of the city. But then, his concern was not really with the past but with the future and his problem was to find a vantage ground for envisioned futures. Perhaps he sensed the spreading cultural neurosis in Asia and Africa, in response to the pressures to live by Europe's past rather than one's own, to avoid accusations of revivalism or conservatism.

Happiness

'What good is happiness if it cannot buy you money?'
—Attributed to Zsa Zsa Gabor

In 2007, one of Britain's leading schools, Wellington College at Crowthorne, announced that it would offer classes on happiness to combat materialism and celebrity obsession.[1] The following year, the *New Scientist* summarized the results of a sixty-five-country survey that showed that the highest proportion of happy persons lived in, of all places, Nigeria, followed by Mexico, Venezuela, El Salvador, and Puerto Rico. It is true that happiness surveys differ in their findings. According to one set, happiness has much to do with prosperity, levels of development, or health care; according to

---

[1] www.wellingtoncollege.org.uk. Also see Alastair James on 'Wellington College Extends "Happiness Lessons" to Parents', The Telegraph, 20 September 2010.

another, these things do not matter. It is the second set that has produced countries like Vanuatu, formerly the happiest country in the world that most of us have not heard of, and another world champion in happiness, Bangladesh, which many of us believed could well qualify as one of the world's unhappiest countries.[2] In comparison, some of the richest nations languish near the bottom of the list.

However, I am not concerned here with comparative happiness or the methodology of studying happiness; I am concerned with emergence of happiness as an autonomous, manageable psychological variable in the global middle-class culture. And the two events can be read as parts of the same story. If the first factoid—discovery of happiness as a teachable discipline—suggests that in some parts of the world happiness is becoming a realm of training, guidance, and expertise, the second reaffirms the ancient 'self-consoling', 'naïve' belief that that you cannot always be happy just by virtue of being wealthy, secure, or occupied. You have to learn to be happy.

Together they partly explain why clenched-teeth pursuit of happiness has become a major feature and a discovery of our times. Perhaps, the other explanations are the growing confidence in some sections of the globe in the power of human volition and the developing technology of human self-engineering as by-products of the ideology of individualism. These changes push many to believe that it is up to them, individually, to do something about their own happiness, that happiness cannot happen or occur, nor can it be given. It has to be earned or acquired. This self-conscious, determined search for happiness has gradually

---

[2] See http://www.thehappinessshow.com/HappiestCountries.htm (accessed on 11 February 2011). This is only an example. The internet is now flush with surveys of happiness. They use different measures and arrive at different results, but I have not come across serious efforts to examine what these differences mean culturally and psychologically.

transformed the idea of happiness from a mental state to an objectified, measurable quality of life that can be attained the way an athlete—after training under the guidance of experts and going through a strict regimen of exercises and diet—gets a medal in an Olympic track event.

In sum, happiness has become a central plank of the global regime of narcissism. It has joined the other better known planks of the regime such as the flourishing cosmetics industry, the incipient but quickly growing industries of immortality and virtual reality, and even the previously escapist but now increasingly narcissistic ventures like alcoholism and drugs.

Some may trace this change in the idea of happiness to the especial style of death-denial encouraged by late twentieth-century capitalism. That would be a simplification. I am inclined to agree with Ernest Becker that there *is* an element of death-denial in all societies—indeed, societies can be seen as systems of death-denial—but some of the more 'successful' capitalist societies seem to have specialized in it.[3] In these societies an obsessive concern with death throws into relief a form of denial that rejects the traditional belief in many societies that the philosophically minded must think of nothing less than death as the starting point of all philosophy. In a fully secularized society, unacknowledged fear of death cannot but be a gnawing presence in everyday life and the idea of an afterlife a fragile defence. We shall briefly return to this issue again.

This is a reversal. At one stage, Protestant ethics, sired by Puritanism and widely seen as the engine of industrial capitalism, sought to purge happiness as a major goal of life. Puritanism tended to equate the search for happiness with hedonism. Karl Marx

[3] Ernest Becker, *The Denial of Death* (New York: Collier-Mac., 1973). This is one of the very few works that seem to see death-denial as a crucial building block of cultures and societies.

recognized this when he called political economy a 'science of wealth' and 'a science of marvellous industry' that was 'simultaneously the science of denial, of want, of thrift, of saving. ... the science of asceticism. The discipline's true ideal is the ascetic but extortionate miser and the ascetic but productive slave.' The second half of the twentieth century saw the collapse of that ideal, perhaps as a consequence of the spectacular death dance in the form of the two World Wars and a number of genocidal revolutions, which broke the older certitudes and forced one to confront a hard, secular idea of transience. The new global regime of narcissism stands face to face to a new, decentralized, fragmented but no less global regime of desperation. The regime of desperation is held together not by any single political or social ideology or metaphysics of a good life but by the psychology of despair.

The determined pursuit of happiness is now seen as a response to a disease called unhappiness. For, in the post-World War II world, unhappiness in some parts of the world has been systematically medicalized. It is now the domain of professionals, where the laity by itself cannot do much except cooperate with the experts. To acquire normal happiness, one now requires therapy, counselling, or expert guidance—from a psychiatrist, psychoanalyst, or professional counsellor or, alternatively, from a personal philosopher, wise man or woman, or a guru. In the post-War era, there were a number of bestsellers by respected scholars, such as Bertrand Russell, Erich Fromm, and Eric Berne, which sought to guide us through this troublesome, unhealthy state called unhappiness and to help us 'conquer happiness', as Russell put it.[4] I am not surprised that such an over-planned, aggressively

[4] Bertrand Russell, *The Conquest of Happiness* (London: George Allen & Unwin, 1930); Erich Fromm, *To Have or to Be?* (1976), *The Art of Being* (1993), and *On Being Human* (New York: The Continuum International Publishing

rational search for happiness produced as its side-effect some rather determined efforts to escape its clutches. To judge by Russell's daughter's memoirs, her schizophrenic brother's illness might have been a direct defiance of her father's mechanomorphic concept of happiness. She in effect wishes that her father had been more open to the less 'scientific' but perhaps more humane school of psychology pioneered by Sigmund Freud and less in awe of the hard, ultra-positivist behaviourism of J.B. Watson.

The trend continues. Only recent guides to happiness are less magisterial. However, they are by no means less popular, whether written by such space-age sages like Deepak Chopra and the intrepid author of the *Chicken Soup for the Soul* series, Jack Canfield, or by their less ambitious versions in the form of agony aunts and quick-fix weekend advisors in newspapers and tabloids. Recently, psychoanalyst Avner Falk sent me the following apocryphal exchange from Jerusalem:

Dear Walter:

The other day I set off for work leaving my husband in the house watching the TV. ... I hadn't gone more than a mile when my engine conked out and the car shuddered to a halt. I walked back home to get my husband's help. When I got home I couldn't believe my eyes. My husband was in the bedroom with a neighbour, making passionate love to her. I was floored. ... I love him very much. ... I feel like my whole life is in ruins and I want to kill him and myself.

Can you please help?

Sincerely,

Sheila

Group Inc., 1997); Eric Berne, *Games People Play* (New York: Grove, 1964). It is unfair to bunch together these diverse scholars, especially the mechanomorphic, soulless concept of happiness in Russell with the now-unfashionable Fromm who probably supplied the first serious social criticism of 'prefabricated happiness', but I am merely speaking here of the rediscovery of happiness as an achievable individual goal and a matter of individual and social engineering.

Dear Sheila:

A car stalling after being driven a short distance can be caused by a variety of faults with the engine. Start by checking that there is no debris in the fuel line. If it is clear, check the jubilee clips holding the vacuum pipes onto the inlet manifold. If none of these approaches solves the problem, it could be that the fuel pump itself is faulty, causing low delivery pressure to the carburettor float chamber, in which case it must be replaced.

I hope this helps.

Walter

છ

Both the disease called unhappiness and its adjunct, the determined search for happiness, seem to target the developed, prosperous, modern societies. Certainly these societies do not usually come off very well in many happiness surveys—one is tempted to guess that only after one's basic needs have been met, following the likes of Abraham Maslow, can one afford to have the luxury of worrying about vague, subjective states like happiness and unhappiness. Alternatively, one can hazard the guess, following Ivan Illich, that only those who have lost their moorings in conviviality and the normal algorithm of community life can hope to learn to be happy from professionals.

This conscious pursuit of happiness, though it came into its own in the twentieth century, is mostly a contribution of the Enlightenment. The belief that one can scientifically fashion a happy life despite hostile environmental factors and what we call random interventions of probability or chance—our ill-educated forefathers called them conspiracies of fate—requires confidence in human agency, rationality, and individual will. Indeed, the search for happiness consolidated itself as a legitimate yearning only in the late eighteenth century, by when the

Enlightenment values had made inroads into the European middle class. The constitution of the United States was the first constitution to sanction the demand for and the pursuit of happiness. But it was a very specific kind of happiness that Thomas Jefferson had in mind. Hanna Arendt says that in the Declaration of Independence, Jefferson personally substituted the term happiness for the term property. She adds that American usage, especially in the eighteenth century, spoke of 'public happiness' where the French spoke of 'public freedom'.[5]

This marked a break. Before the eighteenth century, the predominant mode of seeking happiness was aligned to, and intertwined with, theories of transcendence. And outside Europe that alignment continued. Both the Buddhist concept of *ananda*, which later seeped into the Vedantic worldview, and the Christian concept of bliss had little to do with the new idea of happiness in modernizing West. Ananda or bliss happened. It rarely came to those who searched for happiness. You could, of course, hasten or precipitate it, without actually striving for it, through correct rites and rituals, mystic experiences, meditation, or other forms of exercises in self-transcendence. Happiness of the kind we now associate with individualism and the juridical self has an uncertain status in the non-modern world, more so because some of the major civilizations of the world, such as the Chinese and the Indian, locate their utopias in the past.[6] Given their nonlinear concept of time, the past in these civilizations do have the prerogative and the potentiality to become the future. But, for

[5] Hanna Arendt, *On Revolution* (London: Faber and Faber, 1963), p. 115. See particularly Ch. 3, 'The Pursuit of Happiness.'
[6] The idea of utopias-in-the-past was not unknown to the Judea-Christian and Islamic traditions. The garden of Eden was utopic in many ways, but it had to be rejected in post-medieval Europe as an appropriate utopian vision. It had to learn to survive in an attenuated form and a metaphor the way the

all practical purposes, one has to be reconciled to live in this imperfect world with what Freud once called the normal unhappiness to which we are heir. The past like the future often serves as a social and moral critique of the present.

Indeed, in some Indian texts, the search for happiness is seen as slightly déclassé. Valmiki's Ramayana—others mention other texts—tells us that the benefits of reading the epic are different for different castes. The Brahmins who read it get *gyana* (knowledge), the martial Kshatriyas *kirti* (fame/glory), the business-minded Vaishyas money, and the lowly Shudras get—Chopra and Canfield may be mortified by this—happiness.

ॐ

The expanding sense of human omnipotence and the growing confidence in social and psychological engineering after Renaissance brought a different concept of human agency into play in social affairs. New theologies of the state, history, and science began to talk of building from scratch a 'new man' better suited to human potentialities according to their competing dogmas. A parallel process in psychology firmed up the trend in the late nineteenth century. Almost all of the emerging models of human personality and society promised a this-worldly, non-transcendental version of happiness and were confident that, through proper retooling of social institutions, it could be ensured in the short run. Not surprisingly, once the idea of cultivable, learnt, or achieved happiness entered the scene, many authoritarian regimes in our times, unlike earlier despotisms,

---

idea of primitive communism survives in Marxism—a somewhat tattered, Rousseau-esque, childlike, and childish construct fit for the premoderns and non-moderns.

began to claim that they were pushing their subjects into the best of all possible worlds and began to demand that their subjects be happy.

In such regimes, if anyone claimed to be unhappy, it became a confession of delinquency and his or her normal place remained, officially, outside society. Happiness, like school uniforms, became compulsory. For, not to be happy in a utopia is, by definition, a criticism of the utopia and unforgivable dissent. In the twentieth century, in many societies such dissenters have filled psychiatric clinics and jails. The Soviet Union, for instance, was never secretive about this tacit component of its ideology of the state. The Soviet psychiatrists were mobilized to give teeth to the state's official vision of an ideal society. Nazi Germany did even better. It liquidated such delinquents as enemies of the state.

In Lin Yutang's interpretation of Confucius, for anyone seeking happiness it is important to find a good chair to sit.[7] The gifted Indian philosopher Ramchandra Gandhi discovered this independently. For the last twenty years of his life he was known by his chair at the India International Centre at New Delhi, on which he spent long hours under the portico of the Centre. *Panchatantra*, the ancient Indian collection of folk tales, is only slightly more ambitious. The way to happiness, it claims, is finding one or two good friends. Such modest prescriptions for happiness—a version of the small happiness that cultural anthropologist Tamotsu Aoki commends—are possible only in societies where grander versions of happiness are usually seen as mostly outside the reach of human volition and individual effort. In such societies people are socialized to be happy with odd bits of happiness

[7] Lin Yutang, *The Importance of Living* (New York: William Morrow, 1996).

that come their way. General Eustace D'Souza, an Indian officer in the British Indian Army, who saw action in World War II, was accidentally posted both at Italy and Japan when these two countries surrendered to Allied forces. He recalled, for a now-defunct popular magazine in India, *The Illustrated Weekly of India*, the different responses of the two defeated peoples. While in Italy there were scramble for rations and other goodies being distributed by the victorious Allied army and undignified fights to get larger shares, in Japan even the obviously starving never rushed for food and there was no jostling for rations.

One doubts, if this can be read as a comment on the relative merits of the two cultures or their capacity to withstand deprivation. The difference perhaps indicates that, in some cultures, happiness—or, at least, reduction of unhappiness—is less a matter of personal attainments or gains and more a state of mind associated with community affiliations and social behaviour. Most individuals in these cultures tend to believe that happiness cannot come to one when one functions only as an individual competing aggressively with everyone else and, hence, it is probably pointless to ignore the codes of social conduct to run for individual gains only. One must learn to wait for such gains. Which is probably another way of saying that happiness comes mostly from within a form of inter-subjectivity that has something to do with, what Illich calls, conviviality, not with accumulating, possessing, or becoming.[8]

Appropriately, Aoki pleads that we give up the grand idea of happiness and opt for small ideas of happiness, the kinds that

[8] Ivan Illich, *Tools for Conviviality* (New York: Harper and Row, 1973). This still remains a powerful plea for a robust scepticism towards the reign of professionalism and expertise apart from being an early, if indirect, critique of the happiness industry.

one finds strewn around in everyday life. The smallness itself presumably ensures that the ideas of large, dramatic, organized, expert-guided happiness get lesser play in our lives and are not allowed to overwhelm entire societies by democratic consent, manufactured or otherwise. Such small forms of happiness can even serve as oases within overwhelming unhappiness. In the genocidal battle of Kurukshetra in the epic Mahabharata, which lasted for eighteen days, conventions demanded that the battle begin everyday at sunrise and stop at sunset. At the end of the day, the warriors of the two sides visited each other's camps, exchanged pleasantries, and talked of happier days they had spent together earlier.

The presently dominant idea of happiness, being subject to individual volition and effort, ensures that the search for happiness has a linear trajectory. In that idea, there is always a hope for perfection. Perfect happiness comes when one eliminates, one by one, all unhappiness. This is not an easy task. You cannot, for instance, eliminate death, old age, and many forms of illness and chances of catastrophes. But at least you can live a happy life, the presumption goes, by forgetting them or by denying their existence. All societies institutionalize an element of death-denial. But only in modern societies does that denial take the form of a panicky repudiation of the idea of death itself. Not only because, in the mythos of modernity, there is no genuine place for the idea of a life after death but also because in that mythos there is no admission of a natural limit to individual consumption in death. Death-denial and a debilitating fear of pain are the obverse of the modern idea of happiness.

The changing culture of modern medicine and the contemporary idea of healing have begun to faithfully reflect this connection. Surveying recent literature on the subject, Toby Miller and Pal Ahluwalia draw attention to the way the *British Medical Journal* derides modern medicine for fighting '... an unwinnable battle against death, pain and sickness at the price of adequate education, culture, food, and travel, in a world where the more you pay for health, the sicker you feel, and "social construction of illness is being replaced by the corporate construction of disease."'[9]

∽

There survives another concept of happiness, more nuanced and yet, at the same time, more down-to-earth. It affirms that healthy, robust, authentic happiness—'authentic' in the sense existential psychoanalysis deploy the term—must have a place for unhappiness. Aoki talks about the sadness of unrealized hope and the struggle to acquire a language in which to talk about happiness. In such instances, the presence of the unpleasant does not necessarily mean the diminution of happiness. It becomes part of a happy life that oscillates between the pleasant and the unpleasant, achievement and failure, being and becoming, work and play. In such a life, work becomes vocation and leisure need not be reinvented as the antithesis of work. Vocation includes leisure, exactly as a pleasurable pastime may comprise some amount of work. The idea of perfect happiness is consigned either to the domain of the momentary, or the transient, or to the mythic, or the legendary. It cannot be achieved in life, but may be realized in exceptional moments.

[9] Toby Miller and Pal Ahluwalia, 'Editorial: Psychocivilized?', *Social Identities*, March 2008, 14(2), pp. 143–4; see p. 143. The quotes are from R. Moynihan and R. Smith, 'Too Much Medicine?', *British Medical Journal*, 2002, Vol. 324, pp. 859–60, see p. 859; and R. Moynihan, I. Heath, and D. Henry, 'Selling Sickness: The Pharmaceutical Industry and Disease Mongering', *British Medical Journal*, 2002, Vol. 324, pp. 886–90, see p. 886.

Years ago, philosopher K.J. Shah, simultaneously an admirer of Wittgenstein and Gandhi, found, on reading Erik Erikson's celebrated book *Gandhi's Truth*, the author's concept of a happy marriage problematic. Erikson seemed to believe, Shah said, that Gandhi's relationship with his wife was ambivalent and his marriage less than happy, because the two of them constantly quarrelled. Shah found this concept of marriage strange. According to him, the strength of a human relationship should be measured not by the absence of quarrels, but by how much quarrel the relationship could take. This argument, too, has a parallel definition of happiness built into it—a happy person should be able to bear larger doses of unhappiness. This is not Oriental wisdom, for Erikson's guru Sigmund Freud's Dostoevskyan, tragic vision of life can easily accommodate Shah's definition of happiness. To the first psychoanalyst too, the sense of well-being of a mentally healthy person shows its robustness when the person is able to live with some amount of unhappiness and what is commonly seen as ill-health. This is probably what Freud meant in his famous letter to a patient's mother, in which the intrepid healer advised the worried mother to reconcile herself to the 'normal' unhappiness in her son's life.

Index

About the Author

His interests and curiosity may seem incredibly wide and open-ended to his readers, but Ashis Nandy himself believes that he has only a few persistent and narrow concerns—intellectual and ethical. Such concerns make repeated appearances in his work in different guises. Three of them, he thinks, are particularly pertinent and scaffold much of his recent work. The first is to acknowledge and listen to those silenced or ignored by an iniquitous, arrogant global knowledge system; the second is to look at politics and society through the prism of persons and their selves, to ensure that the human is not overwhelmed by impersonal institutional structures and the so-called larger movements of history; and the third is to explore within cultures—as encrypted in everyday life of ordinary people—to identify possible means of resistance to the mega-projects of the state and of ambitious, apparently space-and-time-defying movements and ideologies claiming privileged or superior knowledge and rationality.

These concerns are interconnected in Nandy's work through an awareness of the politics and cultures of knowledge that have hidden, unacknowledged pasts, from which they have beautifully and elegantly distanced themselves to claim universal validity and to, paradoxically, lead the battle against forms of violence and oppression they themselves have popularized. This paradox comes, Nandy believes, as a by-product of some of the earlier strains of globalization that constitute the dark underside of the presently dominant systems of knowledge globally—the destruction of the indigenous peoples of the Americas, the Atlantic slave trade, forms of colonialism that strutted around the globe with a social-evolutionist concept of progress, some of the ambitious, left-Hegelian revolutions that took a larger toll of their own people than of their enemies, and the two world wars that revealed that not only the context but the texts of science have been contaminated by human cruelty and greed.

Though he has worked for many years on alternative visions of desirable future and is presently working on alternative forms of cosmopolitanism, a large part of Nandy's work is based on an abrasive, wide-ranging theory of negation, based on his assumption that, in matters of public awareness in our times, dystopias have always been more effective than utopias.